LIGHTHOUSE
The Life & Times of McNeil

McNeil

AN ADVENTURE IN THE RCMP

George Garrett

Ⓝ YOUR NICKEL'S WORTH PUBLISHING

The Life & Times of Lighthouse McNeil: An Adventure in the RCMP
written by George Garrett © RCMP Heritage Centre, 2016
All rights reserved

Published by Your Nickel's Worth Publishing.
September 2016

The anecdotes and remembrances contained in this biography are based on newspaper and newsletter articles about Stirling McNeil, and interviews with his friends and family. Any opinions expressed are those of the interviewees and do not necessarily reflect the views of the author, the publisher, or the RCMP Heritage Centre.

Made possible through the efforts of the RCMP Heritage Centre. The publisher wishes to thank the kind assistance of Al Nicholson, CEO, RCMP Heritage Centre, and Media Relations, "F" Division, Regina, SK in the production of this book.

The publisher also wishes to thank visual artist Henry C. Purdy, Charlottetown, P.E.I., for his generous permission to use the portrait he painted of Stirling McNeil, a retirement gift presented to him by "L" Division NCOs, on the cover of this book.

Library and Archives Canada Cataloguing in Publication

Garrett, George, 1934-, author
     The life & times of Lighthouse McNeil : an adventure in the RCMP
/ George Garrett.

Includes bibliographical references.
Issued in print and electronic formats.
ISBN 978-1-927756-65-2 (paperback)—ISBN 978-1-927756-66-9 (epub).—
ISBN 978-1-927756-67-6 (mobi)

          1. McNeil, Alexander Stirling, 1908–2004.   2. Royal Canadian Mounted Police—Biography.
3. Police—Canada—Biography. I. Title. II. Title: Life and times of Lighthouse McNeil. III. Title: Light-house McNeil.

HV7911.M36G37 2016   363.2092   C2016-902230-7
                                                              C2016-902231-5

Cover portrait © Henry C. Purdy. Used with permission.
"Chief Iron Shield" reproduced with the permission of the Estate of Nicholas de Grandmaison.
All other interior images, except where noted © McNeil family. Used with permission.
Cover and book design by Heather Nickel.
Printed in Canada.

Your Nickel's Worth Publishing
Regina, SK

www.ynwp.ca

*This book is dedicated to the thousands of men and women
who have served and are serving in the RCMP.
Their commitment to uphold the traditions of the Force
is appreciated by their fellow citizens of Canada.*

*This is the story of the remarkable career of one member,
Alexander Stirling McNeil, whose accomplishments shine
like a beacon across the glory years of an honoured and respected
organization—the Royal Canadian Mounted Police.*

The policeman must be a minister, a social worker, a diplomat, a tough guy and a gentleman, and of course he'll have to be a genius because he'll have to feed a family on a policeman's salary.

—PAUL HARVEY, American radio broadcaster and policeman's son, author of "Policeman"

CONTENTS

RCMP RANKS: 1931–1966

COMMISSIONED OFFICERS

Commr.	Commissioner
D/Commr.	Deputy Commissioner
A/Commr.	Assistant Commissioner
C/Supt.	Chief Superintendent
Supt.	Superintendent
Insp.	Inspector
S/Insp.	Sub Inspector
	Detective Inspector

NON-COMMISSIONED OFFICERS (NCOS)

CSM	Corps Sergeant Major
S/M	Sergeant Major
S/S/M	Staff Sergeant Major
S/Sgt.	Staff Sergeant
Sgt.	Sergeant
Cpl.	Corporal
L/Cpl.	Lance Corporal

Other Ranks

Cst.	Constable, 1st Class
2/Cst.	Constable, 2nd Class
3/Cst.	Constable, 3rd Class
Sub-Const.	Sub Constable
	Trumpeter & Bugler
S/Cst.	Special Constable
	Marine Constable

Positions of Command

CO	Commanding Officer
OC	Officer Commanding
OIC	Officer in Charge
NCO i/c	Non-Commissioned Officer in Charge

Areas of Command

Div.	Division
S/Div	Sub Division
Det.	Detachment
GD	General Duty
GIS	General Investigations Section
CIB	Criminal Investigation Branch
S&I	Security & Intelligence Branch
Ident.	Identification Section

* Information re: ranks sourced from *Report of the Royal Canadian Mounted Police for the Year Ended March 31, 1936*, Dominion of Canada, Ottawa, ON, 1936 and *Report of the Royal Canadian Mounted Police: Fiscal Year Ended March 31, 1963*, Queen's Printer and Controller of Stationery, Ottawa, Canada, 1964.

THE PERIPATETIC POLICEMAN

FREQUENT TRANSFERS WERE a way of life in the RCMP for many years. Members could not marry in the first five years of service. That gave the Force flexibility in ordering transfers, often with little notice. Stirling McNeil was truly peripatetic—always on the move.

26-05-1931	"Depot" Division, Regina, SK, training
11-07-1931	Regina Town Station, SK
30-01- 1932	Moose Jaw, SK
11-07- 1932	Regina Town Station, SK
21-07- 1932	Prince Albert, SK
23-07- 1932	Waskesiu, SK
27-03- 1933	Melfort, SK
06-06- 1933	Waskesiu, SK
26-07- 1933	Prince Albert, SK
31-07- 1933	Duck Lake, SK
14-08-1933	Prince Albert, SK
20-09-1933	Shellbrook, SK
02-02-1934	Big River, SK

14-02-1934	Shellbrook, SK
28-02-1934	Melfort, SK
01-07-1934	Fort Simpson, NWT
18-06-1936	Fort Providence, NWT
01-09-1937	"Depot" Division, Regina, SK
01-05-1938	Montreal, QC
01-06-1938	Moncton, NB
20-12-1938	Camp Borden, ON
07-01-1939	Trenton, ON
12-05-1939	Rockcliffe, ON
06-06-1939	Fort McMurray, AB
01-09-1940	Rockcliffe, ON
15-12-1944	Saskatoon, SK
13-11-1945	Young, SK
08-11-1946	Biggar, SK
18-01-1948	Edmonton, AB
29-11-1951	Ottawa, ON
15-12-1951	Edmonton, AB
22-12-1951	"Depot" Division, Regina, SK
01-08-1952	Rockcliffe, ON (Musical Ride, secondment)
01-11-1955	"K" Division, Peace River, AB
01-09-1959	"L" Division, Charlottetown, P.E.I.
09-02-1966	Retired to pension

FOREWORD

by Supt. E.C. MacAulay (Rtd.)
BBA, MBA, LLB

THIS IS A book that needed to be written and we owe a debt of gratitude to George Garrett for willingly undertaking the task of assembling the information and organizing it into a chronological account of the life of a great Canadian. It would have been a significant loss to Canadian history not to have created a permanent record of the life of Supt. A.S. McNeil, who was a truly remarkable Canadian, and whose life can be a model and inspiration for others.

Stirling McNeil's life as labourer, athlete, pilot, senior war-time intelligence officer and member of the RCMP encompassed an incredible breadth of activity as well as geography, and through it all there was a remarkable level of caring, humility, acceptance of others, loyalty, dedication to duty, good citizenship, good humour, and a truly remarkable level of ethical conduct. He set a standard well worth studying and emulating.

George Garrett is a most worthy person to have given us this account of the life and times of "Lighthouse" McNeil. An investigative journalist for over four decades, George earned an unequaled reputation among law enforcement personnel as someone who could be trusted with any information, which would only be disclosed at the correct time and for the correct reasons in the interest of justice.

I want to thank George for providing us with this worthy addition to Canadian history and also the RCMP Heritage Centre for pursuing publication of this book, and making it available as an example of the type of citizenship that all ought to strive for.

INTRODUCTION

THE ROYAL CANADIAN Mounted Police have been an integral part of Canada's historical and cultural landscape since 1873, helping to form and protect our great nation, and playing a significant role in creating the Canadian identity. It is the mission of the RCMP Heritage Centre, located at "Depot" Division in Regina, Saskatchewan, to share the stories of the RCMP.

This is one of those stories.

Alexander Stirling McNeil, born in Winnipeg in 1908, joined the RCMP on May 26, 1931. He trained at "Depot" Division in Regina and was posted to a number of detachments in the Northwest Territories, New Brunswick, Québec, Alberta and Saskatchewan. Rising through the ranks, McNeil had no fewer than 34 postings. His career included service in the RCAF during the Second World War, "Air Division" in the RCMP, and OIC of the Musical Ride in 1952. In 1959, then-Inspector McNeil was given Command of "L" Division, the province of Prince Edward Island. The position was later upgraded to the rank of superintendent. He was to remain in that position until his retirement on January 9, 1966.

Upon retirement, Supt. McNeil moved with his wife Carolyn to Vancouver Island. His failing health prompted their final move to Langley, B.C. where he died June 23, 2004 at age 95.

JOINING THE RCMP

In 1931, Canada was in the grip of the Great Depression. While all the country suffered, the regions and communities hardest hit were those dependent upon primary industries such as farming. In the three Prairie provinces the wheat economy collapsed.

Stirling McNeil finished his education at Brandon Collegiate Institute in Manitoba in 1927 and went to work immediately at the local Massey Harris plant, which had begun building reaper-thrasher combines. After working there for several months, he applied for a job at General Motors in the parts and service department in Winnipeg. It was there he got his first taste of football, playing for the Winnipeg Argos—a junior rugby team.

Growing up in Brandon, he had never seen English football but played a game on a dare and made the team. The Argos were beaten by the Regina Pats, who went on to win the Canadian championship. McNeil later moved to Calgary, Alberta where he played for the Calgary Tigers, a senior team. They won all their games but lost the championship, again to Regina, on a cold, icy day that fall.

In 1929, the year of the stock market crash, McNeil received what he called "an ugly call." He was out of a job. In the fall of 1930, with about three days' notice, the General Motors plant was closed and all employees were laid off indefinitely. McNeil was offered a job by the Investors Syndicate but didn't take them up on it because people had taken such a beating in the stock market.

Nevertheless, Stirling McNeil was one of the lucky ones. He moved to Lethbridge, Alberta where he landed a job driving an oil truck for Imperial Oil. That job led to a very embarrassing moment. He was driving one of the largest gas delivery trucks in the fleet, making deliveries across Southern Alberta and forgot to check the gas gauge. He ran out of gas about two miles out of Lethbridge.

My tanks were drained dry. I knocked on the door of the nearest farmhouse, but found that farmer used distillate and I was afraid to put that in a comparatively new engine. I phoned into the office and one of my companions brought a car down, took a can out of the trunk and put some gas in my truck. I got the engine started but I was never so embarrassed in my life.

During this time, McNeil played softball on the Mounted Police team. "They were usually short a player with members away on escort and I got to play every game." After one game, the Sergeant Major—whom McNeil recalled as S/M Pearce—asked him if he was interested in joining up; word had come from Ottawa that the Force was taking on new recruits.

McNeil had already given it lot of thought and, impressed by the quality of the men he knew from the team, was quite interested in the prospect. The Sergeant Major told McNeil to come down to the office the next day, and he would give him "the dope and the data on how to join the Force." McNeil thought he would have no problem passing the medical exam. He was a healthy young man who had grown to a height of 6′4″. But he also needed references. McNeil was asked if he knew Judge Jackson. Indeed, he did. He had asked Judge Jackson to serve on a football committee. Did he know the local MP?

"Oh, yes," said McNeil, "the Brigadier is my doctor." [1]

Both the judge and the MP gave McNeil recommendations, which, he said, were very helpful.

The possibility of a secure job in the midst of the Depression was undoubtedly a consideration. Stirling McNeil had not been born with a silver spoon in his mouth. His paternal grandparents lived in the Eastern Townships of Québec. They were dour, hard-scrabble farmers who lived a difficult life. McNeil's father had gotten out of Québec and come west. But it didn't save him from a hard life. McNeil's father was a conductor for the Canadian Pacific Railway but he was a drinker, too, which broke up McNeil's parents' marriage for a time.

And so, though unmarried and only 22 years old, Stirling McNeil had responsibilities far beyond those of most single young men. His parents had separated when he was younger, and his mother died when he was 19, so it fell to him to help support his two sisters. And thus it wasn't so much the thought of a fine career or that police work was a noble profession, but more the realization that he'd get three square meals a day and clothes to wear and something to put in the bank that sparked McNeil's decision.

---

1   Brigadier John Smith Stewart.

But, as many recruits have found, joining the RCMP was not quite as easy as McNeil may have first thought. He was in excellent physical condition but soon learned that he was just a little too heavy when the police doctor put him on the scales and found that he weighed 176½ pounds.

The doctor told him, "I'm afraid I'll have to reject you: the maximum weight for recruits is 175 pounds—because of the horses they use in training, you know."

McNeil had already given up his job at Imperial Oil in Lethbridge and persuaded the doctor to give him a chance to lose weight over the weekend. McNeil cut down on what he ate and borrowed a training suit from a punch-drunk former boxer named Lee Tessler, who had been a sparring partner for Jack Dempsey in a fight in Shelby, Montana, just south of Lethbridge. McNeil knew Tessler pretty well; this fellow whose nose spread across his face was often seen running around Lethbridge wearing a rubber suit in order to lose weight. McNeil asked if he could borrow the suit for the weekend.

Tessler responded, "Sure, Mac, help yourself." So McNeil got the suit, wiped it out, and dragged it on.

He ran for miles in that rubber suit, the sweat pouring off him, and took a laxative the night before the weigh-in. He didn't have breakfast that morning either. The police doctor weighed him and, lo and behold . . . the scales registered 174½ pounds. The good doctor sent him over to the Orderly Room to be signed on, but first McNeil took a detour to the mess where he wolfed down a huge breakfast. He was *ravenous*. He ate such a big breakfast he thought he probably regained the weight he had lost. But he had met the weight requirement and he was in.

He was sworn in by Insp. W. W. Watson, whom he came to regard as a "very nice gentleman." The effective date of his engagement was May 26, 1931. The intake date should have been May 23, but McNeil told the Inspector he had never been to the Waterton Lakes area of Alberta and was hoping for an extra couple of days before reporting to "Depot" Division in Regina, Saskatchewan. The kindly Inspector stroked out May 23 and wrote in May 26.

McNEIL SET OUT for Regina on May 26, a terrifically hot day. It was a good thing he had two spare tires in his car because he had a couple of punctures and a blow-out en route. The trip took all day and changing tires in the hot sun took its toll. On the western outskirts of the city, about a mile away from "Depot," he pulled into a bluff and decided to take a nap before presenting himself at the barracks.

It was early evening and he fell into a deep sleep, only to be awakened by a trumpet call near daybreak. Hurriedly, he got the car started and drove up to the barracks. He wheeled onto the square and pulled up in front of "A" Block just as the stable parade was moving off.

Not many recruits reporting for training had their own cars in those days—most were met at the bus or train station and delivered to the barracks by the duty driver from "Depot"—but the thing that got McNeil off on the wrong foot wasn't his early morning arrival by car; it was a ten-gallon hat acquired at the Calgary Stampede.

As I was carrying my stuff from the car into the barracks, my hands were full so I just plunked the cowboy Stetson on my head. Well, the riding instructor, Bill Stephens, saw this and remarked, 'I see we've got a cowboy with us; we'll have to see how he does on the Ride.' I could have eaten that hat because it caused me a lot of grief. [2]

And McNeil did have difficulties with horses. On one occasion he was given an old nag of a horse. He tried to put the horse over a jump and got bucked off, hitting his head on a crossbar and knocking him dizzy for a few minutes.

When he picked himself up, the riding instructor came over to him. "Come on, there—you can't go over that jump unless you've got lots of guts."

McNeil got up, mad as a hatter, and retorted, "You get off that horse and I'll show you what guts I've got!"

This was impertinence that instructors simply would not tolerate. Stephens told McNeil in no uncertain terms to get back on that horse right away or be charged with disobeying an order. But Stephens eventually seemed to take a liking to the tall recruit.

Years before, McNeil had worked in Winnipeg with a girl named Lil Coulter. Lil really liked a certain Mountie: Bill Stephens. McNeil now asked Stephens if he knew the girl.

"Yes," said Stephens, "she is my fiancée."

McNeil replied, "Yes, I know her too and she's a very, very fine

---

2   The western riding habits of recruits who were used to working with farm horses were the bane of a riding instructor bent on enforcing the English riding standards required by the RCMP—so showing up in a ten-gallon hat from the Stampede likely didn't do much to endear McNeil to Bill Stephens!]

girl, and if I may take the liberty of saying so, she's much too good for you."

The riding instructor started to laugh.

From then on we were fully reconciled and every once in a while [Bill] would say out of the side of his mouth, 'Just heard from Lil today and she said she wished she had married you.' Well, Stephens and Lil were later married and had a happy life, raising three children.

McNeil's experiences with horses during training were not always the best, and no one could have imagined that one day he would lead the famed Musical Ride on an international tour.

McNeil's experience in working with trucks, however, stood him in good stead at "Depot" Division. An old truck used for hauling baseball equipment to games often broke down and McNeil would somehow get it going again. On one occasion, the CO's car, a Studebaker 8, kept stalling. The two officers in the back were off to a civic funeral but the driver couldn't get the car started.

A supercilious English chap, the driver responded to McNeil's offer of help with, "No, get the hell away from here; you don't know anything about it."

But McNeil knew from the smell of gas that the carburetor had already flooded.

One of the officers rolled down the window. "Well, Constable, you just go ahead and do what you can. We're in a hurry and you probably know more than this chap does."

McNeil lifted the hood and saw that the major lead to the

distributor was loose. He pulled out his jackknife and fixed the wire, but wasn't too quick about it so as not to embarrass the driver further.

After a moment or two, he told the driver, "Now, start it up and I think it should go."

It started easily and the driver glared at McNeil in consternation. Again the officer rolled down the window. "Thank you very much, Constable."

McNeil thought no more about it but later learned a CIB plain clothes member had taken an officer home from a function and decided that, instead of turning the car in, he would pick up his girlfriend and take her to a country dance. Unfortunately, he was involved in an accident, crushing a fender. He brought the damaged car back to barracks, unaware that the other driver involved in the accident had already reported it. After the subsequent investigation, the CIB member was suspended from duty and charged with taking a car without permission.

So McNeil suddenly had new duties. He was taken off the Sergeant Major's Parade and advised that since he had some knowledge of cars, he was now the CIB driver. This meant he would be wearing plainclothes. He asked what would happen to his training, but was told, "Oh, you'll get your training; you can borrow your troop-mates' notes." Most of the exams were already over by this time, but in his spare time, he studied the notes of his troop-mates (most of which he said were better than his own), and he passed the remaining exams.

In McNeil's day there were no formal ceremonies, no "pass-out" parade.

We'd go down to the sports field and the officers would come and inspect us. We were given our marks back and that was it. Every day we'd do chores and stable parades. At the noon parade, the Sergeant Major would come out with a list and say, Jones and Smart, you are hereby notified that you're on transfer to Edmonton. You'll take the six o'clock train tonight. Get your bags done this afternoon. You can have the afternoon to pay your bills but have your bags down by five o'clock and McNeil will take you down to the railway station in the truck.'

There was no posting *en bloc*, either. Newly minted officers left singly or doubly, and it wasn't long before most of the graduating troops were pretty well spread out.

McNEIL HAD NOT yet been posted when his driving skills were once again put to use. The Sergeant Major ordered McNeil to dress in brown serge and report to the officer's mess at eight o'clock. He was told to bring a light kit because they didn't know how long he would be away. He was to join a horse-buying expedition headed by Supt. Spalding, OC Saskatchewan District, which also included Insp. Cumming and a veterinary surgeon. McNeil had maps but Supt. Spalding said he knew where they were going and that they didn't need them. Knowing firsthand that Insp. Cumming would be a nervous passenger, this assurance didn't do much to lessen what would be a bit of an awkward situation.

About ten days earlier McNeil had just come in from late duty when he got a call in the guard room saying that there was trouble at the receiver-general's office in downtown Regina. He was told not to waste any time in responding and was advised to take his revolver with him. McNeil raced to get his revolver and the car. He picked up Insp. Cumming, the financial officer, and tore off for city centre. The car hurtled toward the Albert Street underpass, only to find that:

Lo and behold, the underpass under the bridge was flooded, filled with water. One car had stopped on one side. Another came along and stalled, plugging both lanes of the underpass.

McNeil took one look at the situation and, since this was an emergency—a possible bank hold-up in progress—and there wasn't a pedestrian in sight, went for the sidewalk, the nervous Inspector yelling, "No, no, no!" the whole time.

Nevertheless, McNeil bumped the car down the sidewalk and made it to the receiver-general's office. In the meantime, however, the office manager had called in to say there was no sign of a hold-up or anything else. It was just that the power had gone out, which had apparently triggered an emergency light. McNeil cautiously returned to the barracks, having been admonished by the nervous Insp. Cumming over his "reckless" driving.

The next day McNeil was summoned before Supt. Tate for an explanation.

Well, I was told to get down there as soon as I could. There was some kind of emergency. I didn't know if it was a bank hold-up or not, but I did what I thought was best. Had I known what the situation was, with two cars stuck in the underpass, I certainly would have taken the other way around, but even if I had done so, it might have taken too much time and the emergency would have been over. I realized I could get through (on the sidewalk) and in the best interests of efficiency, I got through.

Fortunately, the Superintendent only laughed and said he thought Insp. Cumming, although a nice chap, was a bit of an old woman anyway. And so young McNeil was told to "just carry on."

Now, here he was on a horse-buying expedition with Supt. Spalding in the front seat and a very anxious Insp. Cumming in the back. Supt. Spalding knew the roads well because he had once ridden horseback through the area and they were soon on their way.

There had just been a cloudburst when they called in at one ranch and the roads were muddy. Supt. Spalding stepped out of the car right into a mud hole, sinking up to the spurs on one of his boots. McNeil had a rag in the car and offered to clean the Superintendent's boots. But Supt. Spalding took the rag from him, saying, "Nobody polishes my boots."

McNeil admired the Superintendent's spirit.

As is typical on the Prairies, the rancher invited the RCMP officers into the house, saying, "You're just in time for dinner."

After visiting several ranches and negotiating the purchase of a number of horses, Insp. Cumming wrote out a cheque as a down payment and the group drove back to the main highway. That was when Supt. Spalding suggested a visit to the detachment in Morse. "There's a new Irish chap there that I'd like to see. He's been doing some pretty good work."

McNeil didn't know the town of Morse but he saw a flag flying and guessed it was the RCMP detachment. As he pulled up, he took note of the police car parked alongside the building.

Supt. Spalding told him, "Get out, McNeil, and see if he is in."

And so McNeil went to the front door and pounded and pounded. It seemed no one was there, despite the presence of the police car. Finally, he heard movement inside. A moment later he was face to face with a man in his underwear.

McNeil told the man he had visitors, but the man said, "Tell them I've been out all night and I'm not available."

McNeil turned to relay this news to Supt. Spalding and almost knocked him over. The Superintendent had come up to the front door himself.

Spalding banged on the door too. "Open up, man!" Then the Superintendent proceeded to walk in.

Cst. Joe Armstrong, the Irish chap, jumped to attention. As he banged his foot down, his privates fell out of the front of his underwear.

Undaunted, Supt. Spalding looked down fleetingly and said, "This is just an inspection. There is no kind of presenting arms or royal salute."

With much chagrin, Armstrong quickly stuck the offending member back in his underwear.

Seeking distraction, Supt. Spalding looked around the office, spotting one or two empty beer bottles on the desk and a couple more in the wastebasket. "What's this?"

Cst. Armstrong hastened to explain that a bank manager who

was being transferred had dropped in to say goodbye and have a drink with him.

The Superintendent looked at his watch. "We're going to go have coffee. We'll be back here at precisely one o'clock and I want to see this place looking better."

Upon their return, Cst. Armstrong was resplendent in red serge and polished boots. The office had been tidied and McNeil could see where Armstrong had given the place a quick scrub—some of the corners were still wet. Still, everything was now spotless and shipshape.

Supt. Spalding asked to see the books, initialed them and indicated to McNeil that he should leave. As he did, McNeil heard the Superintendent tell the Constable to grab a chair and proceed to chat with him about some interesting case.

When they drove away later, Supt. Spalding said about the young Irishman. "A very smart chap—I think he'll do well."

The return trip to Regina was not without adventure either. McNeil was trying to drive circumspectly in deference to Insp. Cumming, so as not to invoke another charge of reckless driving, but just as Supt. Spalding was encouraging McNeil to "move along, move along," some "yahoo" came out of nowhere and whipped down the road, passing them in great style.

Supt. Spalding told McNeil, "You'd better let me drive. I'm not going to eat anyone's dust."

You should have seen the horrified looks on the faces of the passengers in the back seat as we changed places going at a pretty good clip.

One of them, of course, was poor Insp. Cumming.

After a few more miles, Supt. Spalding told McNeil, "You take over now."

That horse-buying trip, was, all in all, quite an experience.

McNEIL AND HIS troop-mates had one last laugh at the member they considered supercilious, the Englishman whom McNeil first encountered when he helped get the stalled Studebaker 8 going. It seemed like the man was disliked by nearly everybody, which wasn't helped by his desire to get out of the "filthy hole" where he was serving (a not-so-subtle reference to Regina). He intended to purchase his discharge and return to England and therefore put in a transfer request to go to Vancouver, believing the Force would do the exact opposite and send him to the east end of the country.

An Irishman by the name of Clancy, a big solemn fellow, hated the Englishman's guts.

Clancy was a very solid, woody guy but didn't have too much detachment experience. He worked in the office for most of his service. I'm sure Clancy tipped somebody off about the Englishman's plans because when the posting did come through, it was to Vancouver.

As soon as the Englishman found out he was livid. Vancouver instead of Halifax, where he would be halfway home. But the sarge came and told him, "You've got two choices. You can either go home through the Suez Canal or the Panama Canal."[3]

---

3   Clancy was later posted to what had been a busy detachment but soon after he got there, reports stopped coming in. Someone was sent to investigate. They found Clancy with his feet up on the desk, spurs on, talking to a couple of ranchers. McNeil figured that was because Clancy didn't want his feet to slip off the desk.

Clancy was a very big, stout man and his uniform "bubbled over." He had a laid-back way of investigating crime, telling the ranchers, "You go ahead and find whoever stole those cattle. Let me know and I'll go out and arrest him."

While in the Force, Clancy learned that he was in a line for a title back in Ireland. He left the Force on pension. Sometime later, when McNeil was on leave visiting Great Britain, he looked Clancy up. Clancy had indeed become a nobleman. But it wasn't as good as it seemed. Two deaths in the family, one on top of the other, meant that inheritance taxes had pretty well cleaned out the estate and Clancy had been left with nothing but the title.

McNeil found it hard to get away. Clancy was homesick for Western Canada and his days in the RCMP.

THE EARLY YEARS

BEFORE JOINING THE RCMP, Stirling McNeil played football with the Winnipeg Maroons, forerunner of the famed Blue Bombers. While in training with the RCMP in Regina, he was invited to play for the Saskatchewan Roughriders in 1931.

1930s Regina Roughriders sweater. The team colours were then black and burgundy, not the now familiar green and white. *Photograph (2001.56.01), courtesy of the Saskatchewan Sports Hall of Fame.*

But the football team had to make some promises to the Force if he was to be allowed to play. The Riders had to sign a waiver with the Mounted Police: if they broke him, they had to fix him, because he was Mounted Police property.

At 6′4″, McNeil was an imposing receiver, one who should be easy to find by a quarterback looking downfield for a target. He returned to the huddle after one particular play in which he had not been thrown the ball, and protested to the

1931 Regina Roughriders.
Photograph (1981.8.25), courtesy of the Saskatchewan Sports Hall of Fame.

quarterback, "Why didn't you throw the ball to me? I'm like a ruddy lighthouse out there!"

From then on, McNeil was known to many of his colleagues on the Force as "Lighthouse McNeil," although Supt. Bill MacRae (Rtd.) recalled he was also known as "Lofty."

The Regina Roughriders were heading to the Grey Cup that year but McNeil could not join them; his supervisor refused him a weekend pass because he had been absent almost every previous weekend playing away-games. And so Lighthouse McNeil missed the resounding 22-0 defeat the Riders were dealt by the Montreal Winged Wheelers.[5]

---

5   "Grey Cup Winners," CFL Hall of Fame. http://cfhof.ca/grey-cup-winners/. Accessed March 17, 2016.

THE ONLY OTHER time he missed a game was on Sept 29, 1931, during a coal miners' strike in Estevan, Saskatchewan.[6] McNeil was ordered one evening to pick up a Sergeant, a bunch of stores, extra munitions, flares, tear gas and protective equipment. There were gas grenades, a protective vest[7], and a few shotguns. They threw everything in the trunk of the car and headed to Estevan. In the car with McNeil were Insp. Moorehead, a Sergeant, a Corporal and a Senior Constable.

We weren't there for long. In a couple of days we set up our head-quarters in downtown Estevan. We had a small office near the town hall, on the second floor. The fire hall was in the basement.

---

6 "In the summer of 1931, 600 men and boys worked in the almost two dozen underground mines of the Souris coal Fields of southeastern Saskatchewan. They laboured ten hours a day in subterranean coal seams sometimes not big enough to allow a miner to stand up. In the Crescent Mine and Eastern Collieries, one to two feet of water routinely collected in the work areas. Western Dominion Collieries was notorious for not replacing damaged or rotted timbers, and roof cave-ins were frequent. Many of the underground mines had totally inadequate ventilation; smoke from blasting hung in the air like a fog. 'Black damp'—high concentrations of carbon dioxide—plagued many of the mines and regularly made the workers seriously ill. 'Refuge holes,' which offered miners some protection during a fire or cave-in, were few and far from the coal face.

"For working in these harsh and dangerous conditions miners were paid 25¢ for each ton of coal that they dug, hand-loaded on coal cars and pushed to the main shaft. An experienced miner working hard for the whole of his ten-hour shift could earn $1.60. Dockage for rocks, clay and small-sized coal further reduced his take-home pay. Miners were also obliged to do extra work such as laying track, timbering, pumping water, and clearing up roof falls, for which they were not paid. Coal miners' wages in Alberta and British Columbia exceeded those paid in Saskatchewan by 50% in the decade between 1921 and 1929. Despite this, the Estevan–Bienfait area mine owners implemented sizable wage cuts in 1931."

Garnet Dishaw, "Estevan Coal Strike," *Encyclopedia of Saskatchewan*, http://esask.uregina.ca/entry/estevan_coal_strike.html. Accessed May 4, 2016.

7 Bulletproof.

McNeil worked in plainclothes, mingling with the local people, "kind of listening to what was going on at the mine just out of town," then reporting it back to fellow RCMP members.

All of a sudden a strike exploded, with all these miners marching on the town. It was a bloody melee, to say the least.

Mounties used riding crops to defend themselves from the stones and bricks being thrown, and a lot of people were badly injured. One member was stationed in the office to guard the munitions. His Sergeant told McNeil to call Insp. Moorehead and tell him to send reinforcements to the town hall immediately. The Inspector left the phone dangling in the office and yelled for backup. Policemen piled into cars to rush to the scene.

As Insp. Moorehead and his team arrived, the mayhem was well underway. When Insp. Moorehead saw that things were getting out of hand, he said, "We'll fire one volley over their heads." In those years, nobody in the RCMP dared even to reach for their revolvers, and the rioters apparently thought police would never draw their guns. One said something like, "See, I told you. They're afraid to shoot."

One RCMP member got on the fire truck and pulled it out of the building in preparation for hosing down the miners to quell the riot. When the volunteer brigade arrived, they got the hose ready, but before they could turn the water on, a couple of rioters ran up with axes and cut the hose. McNeil rushed toward the fire truck. One of the men now stood on the seat of the brand new fire engine, axe raised above his head. The glass of the windshield had been folded down and he was about to smash it when someone fired a shot.

The bullet hit the man right in the centre of his chest. As McNeil ran up, the man fell from the seat and over the bumper to land at McNeil's feet. McNeil checked the man over but knew right away, even with his limited knowledge of first aid, that he was dead. "I covered his face with something and that was it." McNeil returned to the front of the fire hall. One of the RCMP members, a man named Palmer, had raised his arm to ward off a blow from an iron bar. The blow broke Palmer's arm. McNeil took off his Sam Browne belt and used it like a lanyard to support Palmer's broken arm while Palmer himself kept hammering away at the rioters with his riding crop, despite the considerable pain he was in.

The Sergeant said, "We'd better get him back to the office. Bring the relief out and bring the tear gas grenades."

"Yes, sir," McNeil replied. He helped Palmer to the office, took off the man's coat and wrapped a magazine around his arm, tying it to form a makeshift splint.

'Now you sit here,' I said. I took his revolver and put it on the desk beside him, with the lanyard still around his neck. I put it on top of the chair and said, 'Now, I'll put the lock on the door. If anyone tries to get in—you know what to do.'

The melee was over when McNeil got to the street, only to find there had been considerable casualties and several killed.[8] As McNeil was driving an injured member to hospital, he was stopped

---

8   A later report said three men died.

by someone who told him to come right away, "a woman's been hit." McNeil quickly stopped the car and told his passengers to stay put as he raced across the street.

Sure enough, there was an English exchange teacher who had been leaning out the window watching the circus when a shot ricocheted off a wall and went right through her ample bosom. Fortunately it only hit her on one side and it went right through her breast, which was bleeding profusely.

They staunched the bleeding as best they could with clean cloths and a towel, cut a rough bandage and bound the woman's chest. McNeil carried her down the stairs and out to the car. There were no seat belts in those days, so he simply told her to hang on and away they went to the hospital. She seemed pretty weak when they pulled up, so again he picked her up and carried her. Others helped too. They put her on a stretcher and McNeil told the hospital staff he thought she should be taken to surgery immediately because she was bleeding so badly.

Later, McNeil looked at his coat. There was a big splotch of blood on the right side of the grey jacket. He did his best to clean it up but it shook him up for a while after that. And even though he took it to a dry cleaner, from a certain angle you could still see the bloodstain for as long as he had that coat.

TALES OF THE NORTH

In 1932, Cst. Stirling McNeil was transferred to a one-man detachment in Waskesiu, Saskatchewan—a great place for McNeil, an avid outdoorsman. He had a birchbark canoe and really enjoyed living and working in that environment.

But it was in this quiet part of Saskatchewan that one of the more colourful events of his career occurred. One morning, McNeil was awakened at about three o'clock—he was told that a drunken man was chasing the camp cook around with a meat cleaver. McNeil arrived while Grey Owl was still in pursuit of the cook, who had refused to make him breakfast. McNeil stepped up, put a police hold on Grey Owl, snatched the meat cleaver from his hands, walked him off to jail, and then went back to bed.[9]

It wasn't to be his last encounter with the noted naturalist and author. Grey Owl was an Englishman who had been a sniper during the First World War. He had been shot in the foot and received a pension as a wounded war veteran. The pension cheque came in the

---

9   McNeil did not tell this story until much later in life when the movie *Grey Owl*,
      starring Pierce Brosnan, came out in 1999. Cam McNeil said his dad casually men-
      tioned, "Oh, Grey Owl? I arrested him. He was a scoundrel."

name of Archie Belaney, and Grey Owl had to go to the RCMP to certify that he was indeed Archie Belaney and could therefore cash the cheque. McNeil knew that Belaney was passing himself off as someone of Indigenous heritage, but to each his own, he thought.

On one occasion, the superintendent of Waskesiu National Park asked McNeil to take food to Grey Owl for his tame beavers. McNeil thought beavers only ate wood and was reluctant to do the job, saying it was a job for the park wardens, not the police. But the superintendent said all the wardens were busy fighting forest fires and asked McNeil to do the task as a special favour. And so McNeil and S/Cst. Wally Laird set out for Grey Owl's home. They finally arrived after their outboard motor broke down, having had to paddle and do several long portages carrying the beaver food. The mosquitoes were terrible.

When they arrived, Grey Owl told the Mounties to put the beaver food off to the side.

But McNeil replied, "No. We'll help you put the food over there."

It was clear Grey Owl was still annoyed at McNeil for having arrested him after the meat cleaver incident. After the beaver food was moved with input from all three men, Grey Owl told the Mounties they could camp out in the yard.

"No," said McNeil "that's not Northern hospitality. The black flies are bad. We're coming in the cabin with you."

Grey Owl was worried that the two men would disturb the beavers, Rawhide and Jelly Roll, who had direct access to the cabin interior through a hole in the floor, but McNeil would brook no argument.

When McNeil was back in Regina a number of years later,

he saw a crowd in a store and, being in uniform, went to investigate. Grey Owl was autographing books. When Grey Owl saw the Mountie, he jumped up, left his admiring fans and surprised McNeil by hugging him as though he were a long-lost friend.

And perhaps McNeil had made a strong impression on Grey Owl. Decades later, while watching Patrick Watson's *The Canadians: Biographies of a Nation*, McNeil learned that Grey Owl had married for the fourth time under the name Archie McNeil of Barra, Scotland—McNeil's name and ancestral home.

Of the man known as Grey Owl, former Prime Minister John Diefenbaker wrote:

> *It would be impossible for me to recall my career as a lawyer without mentioning Grey Owl. He was one of the most memorable men that Canada ever produced. He was a genius; no doubt a charlatan, a poseur and a faker, but no one in North American history ever left behind him such a treasure of concern for what he described as the furred brethren of the soil and his feathered brethren of the air.*[10]

ONE OF MCNEIL's early postings was to the North shortly after the famed episode of the Mad Trapper of Rat River.

Albert Johnson had been sought by the RCMP on suspicion of threatening Indigenous trappers and stealing from their lines near Fort McPherson, Northwest Territories. RCMP headquarters in

---

10 John Diefenbaker, *One Canada: Memoirs of the Right Honourable John G. Diefenbaker, Vol. 1–The Crusading Years, 1895 to 1956* (Toronto: Macmillan, 1975).

Aklavik sent a confidential message to Cst. Edgar "Spike" Millen, delivered by an Indigenous man in a canoe. It said that Johnson had arrived in Fort McPherson on a raft on July 9, 1931 tying up downriver below the settlement and walking to the trading post. He had neither rifle nor dogs, but appeared to be amply supplied with money. The message from Insp. Eames, Officer in Charge in Aklavik, ordered Millen and his men to make inquiries but not to make a special patrol.

Six months later, in December 1931, Cst. A. W. King found Johnson's cabin but was refused admittance. With Cst. R. G. McDowell as backup, Cst. King returned to the cabin and was shot in the chest. It was not a fatal wound.

Just a few days after that, on January 10, 1932, the RCMP sent a second patrol. A 15-hour gun battle ensued, but police still could not remove Johnson from his fortress. When a third patrol arrived on January 19, Johnson had vanished. So began one of the largest manhunts in the history of the RCMP.

A posse of four, including Millen, age 30, searched on foot for two weeks trying to find a trace of the fugitive. The weather was bitterly cold, at times minus 44°. Finally, on January 30, 1932, they found evidence of footprints and followed them to where they saw smoke from a small fire. Johnson had found a hiding place under an overturned tree. The officers and Johnson exchanged gunfire.

Millen got down on one knee and fired. Johnson fired back. Millen fired a second time and Johnson replied with two more shots. With the third shot Millen stood up, turned around and fell face down into the snow.[11]

His fellow officers knew that Millen had been hit but did not know how badly. They did know that if they left him for very long, he would freeze to death. While one officer fired shots toward Johnson's position, the other:

... crawled on his belly in the deep snow for about three metres until he reached Millen's feet. Then he undid the constable's boot laces and tied them together. He used the hastily made handle to drag Millen over to the cover of a bank[12] and out of Johnson's line of fire.[13]

A bullet had struck Millen in the heart. He was dead—and Johnson again escaped.

A posse led by Sgt. Earle Hersey tracked Johnson from Fort McPherson to the country west and north of the Mackenzie River. Johnson was travelling without dogs. On February 3, the RCMP came up with a new innovation—air reconnaissance. The pilot of the Bellanca aircraft, Captain Wilfrid "Wop" May, would become a legend in the North. With his small plane loaded with tear gas bombs, extra ammunition and Cst. W.S. Carter as a spotter, May flew several trips between Aklavik and the wide search area, often bringing food and other supplies to the weary search team.

---

11   Helena Katz, *The Mad Trapper: The Incredible Tale of a Famous Canadian Manhunt* (Canmore, AB: Altitude Publishing, 2004).

12   Snowbank.

13   Katz.

Finally, on February 17, 1932, the posse, with May flying overhead, came upon Johnson. Johnson had been hiding from the RCMP by using caribou tracks to hide his own.[14] Cornered, Johnson made his last stand and gunfire was exchanged. Sgt. Hersey was wounded and the trapper was killed.[15] When the battle was over, May picked up Sgt. Hersey and flew him to Aklavik for treatment.

Another account of the incident said Johnson had been cornered several times but each time he had escaped in a fusillade of bullets, hastening across the frozen, snow-packed hills toward the mountain pass that led to Yukon. When the patrol, unslept and bone-weary themselves, finally caught up with and killed him, they were shocked by the dead man's appearance. Badly frostbitten, emaciated and likely starving—there was only a frozen squirrel in his pack for a meal he would never eat—the trapper was a frightening sight.

A shiver ran through Wop as he looked into the gaunt and gnarled face staring up from the bed of cold snow. The eyes and mouth were open in a grimace as if [he was] in the act of meeting the devil himself, knowing no more peace in death than he had in life. His bullet-riddled body was covered by tattered, worn wrappings, hardly adequate to withstand the winter cold let alone the ravaging forces of the Northern Arctic. Wop half expected him to rise up, shake himself of snow and his pursuers,

14 "Wilfrid 'Wop' May," http://pastyme.uppercanadianheritage.com/index.php/wilfrid_wop_may. Accessed March 16, 2016.

15 Sgt. Hersey was not an RCMP member, he was with the Royal Canadian Signals Radio Station at Aklavik. See: "The Mad Trapper of Rat River" by Nash Neary. http://nwtandy.rcsigs.ca/stories/rat_river.htm Accessed March 17, 2016.

"Beyond the Law," painted by Franz Johnston (Group of Seven).
RCMP Historical Collection, 2006.11.1.

Johnston's famous painting of a Mountie catching up with a criminal in a bleak, northern scene is often mistaken for the legendary demise of The Map Trapper of Rat River, but the artist, in fact, used Sgt. Hubert "Nitchie" Thorne as his model. Thorne served in the Force from 1904–1911 and from 1913–1929. The incident depicted took place near Fort McMurray in 1915. Otto Buschner, a German bushman with great endurance, was wanted for the murder of two men. Thorne, then a Corporal, was the lone officer of the law in the area. He swore in about 30 Special Constables to assist with tracking and capturing Buschner. Cornered several days and 45 miles later, Buschner held a rifle to his head and pulled the trigger, and thus stepped "beyond the law."

"Beyond the Law," *RCMP Quarterly*, October 1961.

and continue his way to wherever it was he had been going before he had become the subject of such a chase.[16]

The final image of the dead trapper was described in equally creative prose by bush pilot "Wop" May:

---

16   Sheila Reid, *Wings of a Hero: Canadian Pioneer Flying Ace Wilfrid Wop May* (St. Catherines, ON: Vanwell Publishing, 1998).

As I stooped over and saw him, I got the worst shock I think I've ever had. Johnson's lips were curled back from his teeth in the most terrible sneer I've ever seen on a man's face. The parchment-like skin over his cheek bones was distorted by it, while his teeth glistened like an animal's through his days-old bristle of beard. It was the most awful grimace of a face of hate I will ever see—the hard-boiled, bitter hate of a man who knows he's trapped at last, and who has determined to take as many enemies as he can with him.[17]

Such were the happenings in the North just before the arrival of Cst. Stirling McNeil. McNeil often flew with "Wop" May, who had served in the First World War and been chased and shot at by the infamous Red Baron. The German pilot was killed by ground fire, which saved May's life.

IN THE NORTH, McNeil served at Fort Providence, Fort Simpson and Fort Liard. He spent his summers on the Mackenzie River and his winters criss-crossing the North on dog sled patrols for as many as 700 miles, earning $2 a day, plus "food, uniform, underwear and toothbrushes."[18] Having not finished high school, McNeil made up for his lack of formal education by reading and studying while on these dog sled patrols. On one such trip, he came across an old trapper who had died in his cabin, frozen solid in the kneeling

17 Frank Anderson, *The Death of Albert Johnson: Mad Trapper of Rat River* (Victoria, B.C.: Heritage House Publishing Co. Ltd., 1991).

18 David Guy, "Adventures of McNeil of the Mounties," *Ottawa Citizen*, July 21, 2001. A11.

position. McNeil and a Special Constable made an L-shaped coffin in which to bury him.[19]

At Fort Providence, McNeil spent a bit of time behind bars, by choice. He had taken a prisoner, who was serving three months, to Great Slave Lake to help catch thousands of whitefish to feed to the dogs. By the time they got back to Fort Providence, both men reeked, and the prisoner was beyond soap and water. McNeil knew RCMP Commr. Sir James MacBrien was coming in by floatplane to inspect the detachment. And "the odour from this fellow was such that I slept in the cell while the prisoner slept outside."

On arrival, the Commissioner commented that this was a most unusual arrangement. "Won't he escape?" the Commissioner asked.

McNeil replied, "I got up and checked him several times during the night. There's no place for him to go, anyway. Besides, we've got a fierce police dog here that terrified the prisoner."

McNeil didn't tell Sir James that it wasn't a tracking dog.

McNeil told the story of Tom Clarke, a most colourful man.

When you'd go to his place, you knew something was going to happen because he was a practical joker. He had a nonsense type of humour. For example, he had these whoopee cushions and he'd sit down and, y'know, they squeak and everything, and make loud noises. You'd touch something and it would fall apart in your hands, and he'd go into gales of laughter. One of Clarke's

---

19   Special Constables were local people, usually Indigenous, who guided and assist-ed the RCMP with many aspects of life and survival in the North.

*tricks was to have a handle just tacked on to a teacup. When you
tried to take a sip, you would spill tea all over yourself.*

Once, the practical joker had the tables turned on him. He had
bought an outboard motor from a travelling salesman whom he had
tricked several times. When the salesman told him how to use the
motor, he told Clarke that he had to keep the spark plug cool by
wetting his hand and touching it. As the salesman left by riverboat,
Clarke started the new motor and followed it out. The salesman
shouted to cool the plug. The shock knocked Tom into the water,
to the delight of all who had been his victims.

THE NORTH COULD be a most inhospitable place, especially in
winter. McNeil told a story of going on patrol down the Liard
River in either 1934 or 1935. It was just before Christmas, and the
temperature plunged to a record -72° F (-58° C).

It was difficult to make progress with the dog team in the incredible cold because the snow crystallized just like sand. At night
they had to make a camp in the open because they had no shelter
to go to.

*Our cheeks were all frozen and later turned black. They just
came up in kind of scabs from frostbite. We slept with our parkas
on and I heard one man's teeth and knees cracking together all
night. I remarked to him that he mustn't have had much sleep
either. He said he had never been so cold in his life, so we both*

got together in the sleeping bags. So we were huddled together
for warmth and, boy, was that ever miserable.

They spent half the night pushing sticks on the fire to keep it going. Normally they would have let the fire go out and re-lit it in the morning. But "by the third day, you're just about played out and bleary-eyed from lack of sleep and exhausted."

We didn't relish a second night out in the cold. All of a sudden, the dogs perked up because they could smell chow and they didn't like being out any more than we did. In the distance we saw lights and, by golly, we moved along, picking up an old trail.

They arrived at a cabin owned by a man named Olie Lindberg. They were not the only visitors. "Wop" May and his mechanic had landed their small plane on the river. May's wife had cooked a turkey before he took off on the flight and put it in the plane. They warmed up the turkey, tossed some frozen fish to the dogs, washed up and sat down to a wonderful turkey dinner.

It was a Christmas he never forgot.

THEN THERE WERE the fall fishing expeditions on Great Slave Lake. But these were no fishing holiday. It was weeks of tedious work.

We'd leave in September and take the barge and police boat to
a joint fishery involving the communities of Providence and
Simpson, fishing at Slavey Point. We'd put out hunting parties

*to see if we could get deer and fish, and, boy, I tell you that was
quite a job.*

The trip would take about a month and a half, sometimes netting a catch of over 30,000 fish. As they caught them, they would set them in caches along the river, covering them with tree boughs. If a trapper came along in need of fish for his dogs, the understanding was that you left a note at the cache to say, "I've borrowed two stakes.[20] I'll repay you sometime." It was the way of the North.

Indigenous people were adept at drying fish, but others were not.

*We bought some dried fish once but it was the damnedest gunk
we ever had. There were boll weevils and everything else, and
we couldn't get rid of it quick enough. We had bought dried fish
with the idea of it being lighter to pack, but the dogs didn't like
it. True enough, it was lighter, but it just didn't work out so I
never bothered with dried fish from then on.*

These fishing expeditions were not for the timid. They used the Indigenous method of fishing with gill nets from dories, nailing sacks across the prow of the boat.

*You could lean across, catch the netted fish with a stick and
squeeze the neck with your hands because the fish would bloat.
Then you grab the fish with your teeth and flip it back overhead.
Then you pull another fish so you could clear a net pretty quickly.
All night your neck was sore.*

---

20   About 20 fish apiece.

You'd have a sharp stick and just push it through and flip it over in this bin. We had willow sticks (cut before the fishing trip began) with one end sharpened to a point. You'd just put the fish on the stick and pile them on.

The men would then stack the fish in rows of about a thousand fish—at times they had rows of several thousand—and loaded them on their barge. The plan was to get the fish down the river without getting caught in ice jams. They always managed to keep ahead of the moving ice floe, but it was nip and tuck at times.

Oh, I never worked so hard in my life and we got less for it in those days. We used to laugh and say if they ever had to work like we did at those fish camps, other guys wouldn't do it. But we enjoyed it. We always used to say, 'Oh well, I'll be out of my brains if I ever go to fish camp again.' But come fall, we would kind of say, 'Let's give it another whirl.'

It was an immense amount of work. Those darn fish were practically worn out by the time we got them in, we'd handle them so often. Stick them, hit them into the stage, then over and stick them, pick them up again on the stage into the boat, then off the boat and into a lighter, cart them along some trail, and so on. We had to pack them high so the animals couldn't get them. We used to take old kerosene drums or gas cans, put them around the bottom of the stage so the animals couldn't shinny up. You'd have to make sure you put them over the snow level and put boughs over them so the ravens couldn't get them. You'd have fish

in your hair, fish in everything else, on your body. You'd go for
a swim [21] *but, of course, the water would be forming ice. You'd*
dash in the water and splash a little water with soap on, then
dash out again.

All that work and the men didn't even eat the fish—they were
fed to the dogs! McNeil never enjoyed fishing after that, even
though he retired to Brentwood Bay, B.C. famous for its salmon
fishing.

McNEIL COULD TALK endlessly about the characters he met in
the North. Gerald Hansen was the manager of the Northwest
Territories at Fort Simpson. He became a Captain in the Canadian
Army and met a pretty little Dutch girl who agreed to marry him.
She could not have known what awaited her in the Canadian North.
Her husband had a chicken coop on his property and somehow
encouraged his bride to crawl in. When she did, a couple of her
husband's friends locked her in.

Here's this poor little soul in the pen, only about four feet high
but you couldn't lift it up and get out of it because it was wired
on all four sides. People came down from the boats and would
look, thinking it was funny. But this little girl was anything
but happy, swearing like a trooper in Dutch, begging the boys
who came out and pointed to her to let her out.

---

21   To try to get rid of the smell and to clean up.

The tourists were amused but pitied the girl. Someone went inside and got her husband. Instead of helping, he burst out laughing.

You talk about a jolly miller, he broke into roars of laughter and kept slapping his knee, tears rolling down his face. Of course, that didn't make him any more popular with his wife.

Mrs. Hansen was finally freed, but relations with her husband were no doubt cool for some time. It took quite a while before she saw the humour of the situation.

One time, Hansen reported to police that someone was stealing gas from the barrel of it he used for his motorboats. McNeil came up with a novel way of solving the crime. He had the owner put sugar in the gas, saying. "We'll damn soon find out who's stealing it."

Sure enough, the next day a bunch of kickers[22] started off to go across the river to Pass Creek. A couple of them got stuck in the centre of the Mackenzie and started floating downriver.

We went to Gerald Hansen and said, 'Do you want to know who is stealing your gas? Do you want to lay charges against them?' Well, Gerald said we didn't have to do anything. He would look after it from here on.

As it turned out, the boaters got a real scare. When their motors seized, they were caught in a swift current and had to revert to paddles, the useless outboards hanging off the end. This worried McNeil, but only for a moment.

---

22   Outboard engines.

If we leave them much longer, they'll float down to Wrigley. And then my thought was, 'Well, maybe that's a damn good thing to do.' Talk about police work, that's kind of a rough brand of justice. Those fellows never came to court. They admitted they had tapped into Gerald's gas, but he didn't want to take any action because they were customers and he figured he'd have them under his thumb come trading time, you see.

WHILE STATIONED AT Fort Simpson, McNeil recalled that the radio set was not working well. If they put a new big battery in it, it would "squawk and spoil everybody else's radio," so they would shut it off. Instead, they would go to the signal station to hear what was happening in the world. Information was printed on a teleprinter and kept for them in chronological order. The signal station reputedly had the tallest flagpole in the Northwest Territories, though it was in desperate need of repair.

Anticipating the arrival of the RCMP vessel, they decided to take the flagpole down before it fell down. They found a man who seemed to know what he was doing and arranged to have the postmaster bring down his team of horses to haul up the pole, using a "deadman" device.

So we got the pole down in good style, easing it down. We had boxes piled up so if the pole went, it would go through the boxes and wouldn't break off. Then we painted it up, put a new pulley on, put a new rope on, and it was time to put it up again.

Well, it's one thing to bring a pole down, it's another to put a massive pole up, as we found out. Of course, we had tarred the bottom and everything else. So finally, we strained with every able-bodied man and woman pulling on the ropes. We had an ingenious system of blocks and tackles. So up it started to go and we got Tiny (the postmaster) to bring his horses. We had finally got the flagpole just about in place when one of the horses started pawing away and fell into what appeared to be an abandoned well.

So here's this horse down the well. We had the flagpole about halfway up and the horse in the well was sinking out of sight. Everybody had to prop up the pole where it was so it wouldn't come down. Our work couldn't be for naught. Then all hands were getting the horse out when we found to our horror it wasn't an abandoned well—it was an abandoned septic tank! And the horse was going down in the goo! Did we ever have a time! Someone made a sling. They put it on a tripod over the horse and finally got it out.

With the horse safe but his rescuers left to deal with the "goo," it was decided they should do something for Tiny, the postmaster who owned the horse. They got him a stiff drink.

AN OBJECT LESSON

In an article published in "The Way it Was … 50 years of RCMP Memories," Stirling McNeil gave his own account of what turned out to be a legendary story. Under the heading "An Object Lesson" McNeil wrote:

> *In 1936, I was posted in charge of Fort Providence Detachment with the exalted rank of acting Lance Corporal whilst employed.[23] One of my first functions was to check over the complaint book entered by my predecessor. I noted repeated complaints of wife-beating by a big Métis man when he was drinking. His wife had taken some terrible beatings. She was prepared to lay charges against her husband, but by the time the Inspector came around on his semi-annual visit when the charge could be laid, she had changed her mind—until the next time.*

---

23   He had taken over from Cpl. Bill Beattie, who had lost his toes on a patrol. Beattie had to be taken to hospital in Fort Simpson, where his toes were amputated.

Well, the next time arrived when word was received that she was being beaten up again. By the time the other member and I got there, the errant husband was sleeping it off. She prevailed upon us not to move him for the time being but said she was definitely going to lay charges against him this time. She had a terrible pair of blackened eyes. Ordinary white people, Métis and Indians were terrified of him when he was drinking.

We got to know the woman because she would bake bread for us after we had several unsuccessful attempts at baking our own. We decided something positive had to be done, so I asked her to let us know as soon as her husband came out of his drunken slumber. She got word to us and we went down. This was largely a Métis and Native community, and there were a number of people there who had congregated because they thought we were going to arrest him. Some excitement was anticipated as this man had terrorized the community when he was drinking and everyone was afraid of him.

I challenged him to put on the boxing gloves with me. He wasn't very happy about it, but with all the people around his reputation was at stake and he couldn't very well back down. Before going North, I had won a regional heavyweight boxing championship.[24] This fellow was just as big, and even heavier than I was, but I knew he didn't have any skill as a boxer. I thought it was time to teach him a lesson. There was always a chance,

---

24   McNeil had earned the title of Light-Heavyweight Champion of Northern Saskatchewan.

however, that I might get knocked out with one of his wild blows, but I thought it was worthwhile taking that chance.

He cleaned up and we all went over to the supply shed where a bunch of willing hands had cleared space for a boxing ring. We both put on the gloves and the Constable who was with me took over as time-keeper and referee. In no time a boxing match got underway, with a capacity crowd of very interested spectators. It had been agreed in advance there would be three two-minute rounds.

STIRLING McNEIL,
GOLDEN GLOVES LIGHT-HEAVYWEIGHT Champion of Northern Saskatchewan.

Well, my opponent took the offensive with a couple of wild swings and I just kept my distance. I wanted to size him up and hoped he would wear himself out. He would make a wild rush at me and I would step aside and land a straight right or left as he went by. I worked him over quite methodically. I talked to him all the while and taunted him a bit in the hearing of his peers about being a bully and beating up on a poor defenseless little woman. I purposely marked him up quite a bit and wound up closing both his eyes. In the last round I picked my spot and knocked him out.

Well, you should have seen the looks on the faces of all the people in the audience, most of whom had been bullied by this fellow for years. They were overjoyed. We revived him and took the gloves off. He was totally subdued and, after shaking hands with him, I said I hoped he had learned his lesson and that there would be no more rough stuff. I warned him that if he ever laid hands on his wife again, we would have another set-to with the boxing gloves.

When Inspector Martin came around on his summer visit, he remarked about the absence of wife-beating complaints. I didn't volunteer any information beyond saying I thought we had the problem solved. The Inspector had obviously heard about it else-where because he said he thought the solution to the wife-beating problem was a good one and that there shouldn't be any more trouble of that kind. This proved to be the case.

Signed,
Reg. No. 10927 Stirling McNeil [25]

---

25 Don Saul, ed., *The Way It Was: 50 Years of RCMP Memories* (Victoria, B.C.: Victoria Division RCMP Veterans Association, 1990).

For years after McNeil left Fort Providence, his successors in the RCMP would warn the wife-beater when he drank that he had better be careful. "Take it easy or Mac will be back." But they didn't have to worry: he was a changed man.

McNEIL FONDLY RECALLED several other characters in the North. One was a man named Brownlee, whom he described as a "real character." He was a Texan, living with one of the local First Nations chief's daughters. Every time the resident Catholic priest made his rounds amongst the flock, he'd try to prevail upon Brownlee to "do the right thing" and marry the girl. But with Brownlee, said McNeil, "It was no dice." By the time McNeil left, Brownlee had quite a little family.

Brownlee was quite a card, and McNeil described him as "a woody devil." Brownlee liked to tell the story of the first time Insp. Martin came to the North, arriving by boat at Fort Simpson. Brownlee asked permission to get a ride upriver to his camp. Because Brownlee had done some favours for the RCMP, Insp. Martin agreed.

Along the way, they pulled into some grassy sward and went ashore for a picnic rather than eat on the boat. Insp. Martin thought it was a good idea to lay out a bedsheet on the ground as a tablecloth. They had pickles, ketchup and other "goodies." Resplendent in his officer's blue uniform complete with brecches and boots, Insp. Martin said: "You know, this is what I like, roughing it, outdoor picnics." The story spread like wildfire. Northerners thought it was hilarious.[26]

---

26 Brownlee was a very outspoken man and once got into an argument with an ex-military man, Colonel Reid, who had been appointed the transportation manager for the Hudson's Bay Company in charge of all the northern passenger and freight ships from Fort Smith down the waterways. Brownlee was a free fur trader and complained that Colonel Reid had deliberately delayed a shipment of goods to him. The argument between Brownlee and Colonel Reid became heated. Reid denied delaying Brownlee's shipment and said it could have been an accident. Brownlee wanted to know what Colonel Reid's qualifications were. *(cont'd.)*

Insp. Martin wasn't the only officer to find himself the subject of ridicule. Although it was hearsay, there was a legend in the North about an officer named Supt. Irvine. It was his first time in the North and he was about to conduct an annual inspection.

Having heard what a "devil's hole" Fort Simpson was, Supt. Irvine was prepared to make his presence known. He had members line up on one side of the men's quarters in the old log house on the hillside at Fort Simpson. He gave them a rigorous inspection and made a number of caustic comments—one member in particular had been "grumping around" in the yard, doing some digging for a garden or the dog corrals.

Then the Superintendent demanded something almost unheard of in that detachment: rifle inspection. Supt. Irvine had been a Sergeant Major and knew a lot about weapons. He was not pleased with what he saw.

"Look at your dirty rifle barrels," he said, "they're as dirty as your fingernails."

Next, the Superintendent encountered a member named King Langfeld, a studious chap and a great reader. He had piled his books on his bedside table and, because mosquitoes were such a menace in the Mackenzie area, had slung a mosquito net over his bed. The

---

As it turned out, Reid boasted a very distinguished record with the British Army in logistics in the Middle East: "Well, I've run boats on the Nile, I had lighters working here and there, and I ran a transportation squadron across the desert."

Brownlee replied, "Well, I've run dog teams in the North, canoes and kickers and everything else, and I still know more about northern transportation than you will ever—period."

That didn't go over very well with Colonel Reid. Reid was seconded to the Air Force in the Second World War and was McNeil's CO at Rockcliffe, in Ottawa for a time. When Colonel Reid realized McNeil had been a Northern man, he took interest in him.

bed was not exactly made according to regimental style. It was in disarray, partly because Langfeld was using a sleeping bag.

Supt. Irvine took one look and said, "Who owns this opium den?" [27]

Irvine continued to find fault, pointing out that it wasn't like "Depot" Division in Regina, and was anything but the members' favourite person. In fact, for many years after, members had a good laugh about all the incidents that happened and how they were all "caught and hoisted on the same rope" by Supt. Irvine.

McNEIL TOLD THE story of another man in the North, who did not have a good command of the English language and had trouble corresponding by letter. Apparently, he wanted a wife. The boys

---

27   The bookworm, King Langfeld, turned out to be an invaluable member of the Fort Simpson RCMP. He had a background in banking and brokerage, but as with so many people during the Depression, he was out of a job and so joined the Force. Langfeld was very proficient in office procedures, unlike most members who had come to the North as big outdoorsmen. But Langfeld was very popular, an out-going type, and often helped members and others in the community with their income tax returns. He didn't charge a fee but would tell trappers who came to him at income tax time, "Come up to the house tonight and we'll split a bottle of booze." After a drink or two, he would tell them, "Well, all right, bring out the damn receipts and everything else, and let's get on with it."

By the end of the winter, liquor was in short supply, so Langfeld decided to make his own behind the stove in the detachment. It was a failure, yet not a complete loss—he ate the mash.

Langfeld was given the job of sub-division clerk, a job that carried considerable responsibility. In those days, the RCMP did just about everything in the community, including the functions of game officer, mining recorder and coroner. "We did everything. We'd bring them into the world (acting as a mid-wife), look after their mining claims and bury the dead." They had to fill out all kinds of reports, not only for the RCMP, but also for various government departments. As was the case with a number of members during the war, Langfeld left the RCMP and joined the Air Force, where he rose to the rank of Squadron Leader.

helped him out by writing to a romance magazine popular at the time. In it was an ad asking for pen pals.

So these young RCMP members wrote a letter for this fellow looking for pen pals. So came spring break and the first plane in, the postmaster swore like a trooper because while the Fort usually got one bag of mail, this year there were about three bags and mostly for this one individual.

When the man came from his isolated community to pick up the mail, people swore even more because while they only got a handful of mail, this person was getting mail from women all over the country. And, according to McNeil, the letters made for "damned interesting reading" all winter. Some of the women were interested in hearing about the Northern Lights. Others wanted to know about their pen pal's financial status. It was a bit of a circus.

Northern men had an affinity for each other and would go to great lengths to help one another.

I had taken over from Cpl. L. J. Hobbs at Shellbrook Detachment so he could go North. He asked me to keep an eye on his fiancée, who was a schoolteacher in Shellbrook. Every time I went by, I would say hello to her or give her a phone call.

Later, Hobbs asked McNeil to be the best man at his impending wedding. His bride-to-be was coming North on the *Distributor* on its first sailing of the spring. McNeil told him he would be happy to do it if he could make it back to Fort Simpson on time. He had been given a new assignment at Christmas, and was to be sent with a dog team and a Special Constable to record mining claims and issue a beaver stamp for licenses, then open a sub-office in Fort Liard—his first command. So taken was he with Liard, when his son was later born, he named him Campbell Stirling Liard.

We arrived in time to see the festivities at Christmas and meet all of the Bands of Indian people, especially the Band of the Nahanni Indians from the mountains. And when the festivities were over, the Special Constable would return to Fort Simpson with the dog team.

McNeil had been "loaned" to the Hudson's Bay Company, which would pay compensation for his time. His office was really just a big heavy suitcase, but he saved on having to gather wood by staying in the Hudson's Bay quarters. He would stamp all the beaver pelts traders brought to the trading post and check their permits. There was talk at the time of a big gold rush coming to the Nahanni and a large number of prospective miners were expected. A few people flew in, staked their claims and got their licenses at Fort Simpson, but the big rush didn't materialize and people did not come down the Liard River as had been expected. Still, McNeil ended up staying for a while.

But he had not forgotten his promise to be the best man at his friend's wedding. Before leaving, he realized he had to get the detachment premises in better shape. The grass in the yard was so high it looked like a hayfield, almost up to the top of the fence and he thought he'd better clean things up in case the Inspector came along. There was so much grass, McNeil decided to set fire to it. However, he cautiously arranged for pails and wet brooms and some help. He was very concerned about fire spreading to the nearby bush.

We very cautiously started a fire guard around the edge of the fence around the detachment and decided to burn it off in between.

Well, all of a sudden the wind changed. Up until then we had a controlled fire, but with the wind picking up, it raced through the heavy grass and headed right for the building. We had a swath of fire there, about five or six feet wide, cleared and burned over but the flames, the embers, were going right into the detachment building.

We worked like fury and had to call for help. I had another fellow go out and round up trappers from the trading post. We beat off the flames, using tubs of water and the brooms. We were very fortunate.

Even with this added excitement, McNeil was able to get to his friend's wedding on time.

Northern men were very special to the RCMP. If you wanted to be promoted; if you wanted to be known as the elite of the Force, you went North. And the North was good to McNeil, a driven, ambitious man.

McNEIL LOVED THE North and its people. One northerner in particular made quite an impression on him: Albert Faille, an old prospector who had always thought there was gold to be found in the Nahanni, an awe-inspiring wilderness now classified as a World Heritage Site and National Park. In 2009, the Federal Government vastly increased the size of the park to more than 30,000 square kilometres. In Albert Faille's time, of course, it was not a designated park, but then as now it cast a spell over those who came to know it.

Stirling McNeil first learned of Nahanni when he arrived in the area aboard the boat that carried supplies for Fort Simpson. McNeil saw an older gentleman with a hunched back place a pack board across his forehead and begin hauling supplies up the steep bank from the boat dock. He offered to give the man a hand, though he was still in his best red serge uniform, as then required by RCMP travel regulations. Faille loaded a 100-pound sack of flour on McNeil's back, and McNeil began the climb up the bank. Soon he was sweating and struggling. To his surprise, the older man—who was carrying two sacks of flour on his back—passed him!

McNeil never forgot Albert Faille and met him years later when he returned to the North. By that time, Faille was in his eighties and famous, the subject of National Film Board and CBC documentaries. He sprang from his bed when McNeil and his son Cam knocked on the door of his cabin. They had not seen each other in years, and McNeil was not in uniform, but Faille recognized him immediately. "Well, Mac!" he said. When he was introduced to the old man and shook hands, young Cam said the old fellow had such a strong grip that it nearly crushed his hand.

McNEIL LEFT FORT Providence in the spring of 1937 and, on leave, decided to see Europe. As was his lifelong habit, everywhere he went, he dropped in to say hello to the local police. This was appreciated in England, Scotland and France, but not so much in Nazi Germany when he dropped in on the Gestapo. McNeil returned to his room to find it in disorder and the lining of his suitcase ripped.

He returned to Canada, a new posting in Regina, and, after a six-year break, back to the Roughriders, which may well be a Canadian Football League record.

THE HEADLESS VALLEY

Few areas of Canada hold as much fascination and mystery as the famed "Headless Valley," part of the beautiful Nahanni wilderness. The macabre name stems from the discovery of the bodies of prospectors who perished in the frigid winters—temperatures at times reach minus 60°. At least two of the dead prospectors were found, allegedly without their heads, on the shore of what became known as Headless Creek. Several other prospectors perished over the years, leading to such morbid designations as the Funeral Range, Deadman Valley, Death Lake, Broken Skull River, Valley of No Return, Vampire Peaks and Crash Lake.[28]

In the years following the Second World War, newspapers were anxious to be rid of war news and were looking for adventure stories. *The Vancouver Sun*'s enterprising editor Hal Straight went all out. He assigned a then little-known reporter named Pierre Berton to fly to the mysterious Nahanni Valley. It was an opportunity too good to miss for pilot Russ Baker, who owned a Junkers monoplane. Baker

---

28 "Nahanni National Park Reserve," http://www.canadianparks.com/northwest/nahninp/page3.htm. Accessed March 16, 2016.

went on to form Pacific Western Airlines but at that time was looking for any free publicity he could get. A third member of the team was *Vancouver Sun* photographer Art Jones, who later became a prominent television personality. Accompanied by a mechanic, the group set out to fly to the Nahanni, complete with banners proclaiming this was the "Headless Valley Expedition." A plane had never landed in that forbidding terrain in the winter, but Editor Straight wanted his story and the expedition embarked in January 1947. Berton soon proved his abilities as a creative writer, radioing back breathtaking stories of the Headless Valley.

The Vancouver Sun, quick to promote the venture, ran an article, "With the Sun's Headless Valley Expedition, Finlay Forks, Feb 7, 1947," before the expedition had even arrived in the Nahanni Valley. The headline, printed in bold-face type, was bound to attract attention: Death Tales Rife in North.

From Finlay Forks, B.C., Berton wrote:

We are in the heart of the British Columbia badlands where the magic word 'gold' makes eyes glitter with a new brightness and lonely men die with their shoepacks frozen to their feet.[29]

The expedition plane had been frozen solid in -37° weather, delaying their departure in what Berton called their "struggle" to reach the South Nahanni River and its Headless Valley—a place where 14 men had perished and, "The will-o-the wisp lost gold mine still haunts prospectors' dreams."[30]

29 Pierre Berton, "With the Sun's Headless Valley Expedition, Finlay Forks, Feb 7, 1947," *The Vancouver Sun*, Feb. 7, 1947.
30 Berton.

With creative prose like that, Berton surely captured the reader's attention. With another 700 miles to go, Berton said people in the hinterland of British Columbia knew no more about the mysterious deaths than the people of Vancouver or Seattle.

They have heard here of the strange, mysterious South Nahanni River, where five men were murdered for their gold, some apparently by decapitation, where waiting winds chill men's souls and an Indian Manitou haunts the mountain passes.[31]

Berton's undoubted ability to create a vision in the reader's eye was illustrated time and again in his prose.

No man here knows the truth about the Nahanni, because no man here has travelled up or even flown over the twisted river where, legend says, mists block the ground from sight.

Berton included in his list of possibly murdered men the names of Willie and Frank McLeod, whose bodies were found in 1905. Legend had it, he said, that they were found without their heads and that was the start of the story of the Headless Valley.

In fairness, Berton did quote a nephew of one of the McLeod brothers, who cast doubt on the "headless" part of the story. The younger McLeod, also named Willie, told Berton he had lived in Fort Liard all his life. He said his uncles were slain and their skeletons were found, wrapped in their blankets, lying by an old fire,

---

31   Berton.

their heads still on them.[32] Nonetheless, the headless bodies myth prevailed for years.

While Berton's stories played up the murder angle, the RCMP had reached a different conclusion. It was likely the prospectors had died of starvation. If their heads were indeed missing, marauding bears were probably to blame.

YEARS LATER, BERTON, by then a famous author of many books, was given a VIP tour of the RCMP "Depot" Division in Regina. His host was none other than Stirling McNeil, who told Berton he had served in the North and knew the Nahanni Valley. Berton told McNeil that he too had been to the Nahanni and had written the story of the murdered prospectors.

McNeil said, "You're wrong, you know. Those prospectors were not murdered. They probably died of starvation, and their heads removed by bears."

Berton insisted he was right. He told McNeil, "I got my information from an RCMP report."

McNeil simply replied, "I wrote the report."

So much for the murder story!

32　Berton.

CAREER TAKES FLIGHT!

As a young Constable, McNeil served in "G" Division (Yukon and Northwest Territories) at such communities as Fort Simpson and Fort Liard, and afterwards as NCO i/c at Fort Providence, Northwest Territories. McNeil was considered pretty handy and operated police boats in both Fort Simpson and Fort Providence. Insp. Martin came through on an annual inspection and said they had to do something with the Mounted Police boat at Fort Smith—it had been involved in an accident. McNeil helped pull the rear of the boat out of the water, installed a new propeller shaft and re-did the bearings, which enabled the boat to complete inspection visits around Great Slave Lake.

It was obvious McNeil enjoyed the experience:

So I took the opportunity of going down on inspection, back down the Mackenzie to Fort Simpson and subsequently to Norman, and then back up the river and the lakes to Fort Rae. There was no Yellowknife detachment then. We were at Reliance and went on to Fort Resolution and back to Fort Smith.

After the Great Slave Lake inspection tour, McNeil was free to go "outside." At Fort McMurray, he met Louis Bisson, pilot of a Roman Catholic Mission plane. In the previous year, McNeil had helped Bisson make emergency repairs to his aircraft, which had been damaged in a hard landing at Hay River. Bisson invited McNeil to fly to Edmonton with him to return the church bishop to Alberta. It was a trip that was to have a significant impact on McNeil's life.

The plane landed on the river behind the Macdonald Hotel in Edmonton, Alberta. Though McNeil was smartly dressed in red serge, he felt flustered at being in the big city after such a long absence and couldn't wait to get out of uniform after the journey. He charged up the steps of the hotel, leaving the bishop and the pilot behind.

There was a young lady at the whirling[33] door of the hotel and I accidentally knocked her down in my anxiety to get in, and out of public view.

The young lady was the woman McNeil would later marry, his beloved Carolyn. McNeil had met her in Lethbridge a few years earlier and recognized her when he helped her up.

McNeil had always had a love of flying. While working for the Ford Motor Company in Calgary in 1929, he took a ground school course with the Institute of Technology but didn't have the money

---

33   Revolving.

to take flying lessons then. The plant where he was employed shut down and he moved to Lethbridge. Shortly after he joined the RCMP, he could afford flying lessons and took his pilot's training in Moose Jaw, Saskatchewan when he was stationed there in 1932. He joined the local flying club along with Cst. Al Lilly, who later became the first Canadian to go supersonic. Emerging from the North in 1937, McNeil learned that the RCMP was about to form an aviation section and he applied to transfer to the new "Air" Division, becoming one of the first members of the Force to join it.

THE RCMP HAD first used aircraft in 1921 to fly a member from Edmonton to the Northwest Territories, but that was on a plane owned by the Imperial Oil Company. The idea of an aviation section grew out of the need for "eyes for the Marine Section" in preventive police work.[34] In 1937, the Force's embryonic aviation section was established with the purchase of four bi-wing, twin engine de Havilland Dragonflys. Having previously relied on the RCAF, the RCMP could now keep an eye on suspected rum-runners in the Maritimes during Prohibition.

On one trip from the Moncton Fair Grounds in New Brunswick, which was used as an airfield before the present airport was built, McNeil spotted the schooner *Nellie J. Banks,* at that time a famous ship. He radioed the Mounted Police cutter, which moved in

---

34   The notion was fostered by Commr. James H. MacBrien, who did much to streamline the Force. Before joining the RCMP, MacBrien had been head of civil aviation in Canada. S/Sgt. D. W. Dawson, later Chief Superintendent and head of "Air" Division, said that MacBrien liked flying and had the foresight to see how aircraft could be very effective in combating crime and carrying out the responsibilities of the RCMP.

RCMP DH Dragonfly, used to spot rum-runners, Moncton, NB.

RCMP DH Dragonfly, used to spot rum-runners, Moncton, NB.
McNeil, a pilot with "Air" Division, is the taller of the two men, centre.

quickly and arrested the crew of the *Nellie J*. Her rum-running career was over.

When McNeil was Commanding Officer of "L" Division in Prince Edward Island years later, he encountered the owner of *Nellie J*. The ship's owner asked McNeil if he remembered the schooner.

McNeil responded that he was the one who had spotted her and turned her in.

"You son of a gun!" said the owner, "You cost me big bucks!"

Many family fortunes were made by rum-running during Prohibition throughout the Maritimes.

RCMP PLANES WERE used extensively in the North for investigations and for flying out people who required hospital treatment. On one occasion in 1945 a sick member of the crew of the famed RCMP vessel *St. Roch* was flown to civilization at the close of the Arctic navigation season. The custom had been for her crew to remain with her when *St. Roch* "wintered in," but with the advent of aircraft they were flown "outside" for duty until the next season's operations began.

The usefulness of aircraft for the RCMP was exemplified by the capabilities of the Ballanca aircraft piloted by Wilfrid "Wop" May in the capture of the Mad Trapper of Rat River in 1932. It was a perfect time for Stirling McNeil, who often flew with May during the years he was posted in the North. McNeil served in "Air" Division from 1938 to 1939, and, as the only "northern" man with flight experience, was chosen as one of the pilots of the first plane operating in "G" Division, covering Yukon and the Northwest Territories. In this role, he oversaw the assembly of the Norseman MK2 CF-MPE airplane in Cartierville, Québec.

At the time, McNeil was working out with the Montreal Alouettes to keep in shape. When the football team's roster was posted, McNeil was on it, but he didn't report for the first game.

The Norseman.

The Norseman.

When the coach called the RCMP to check on the whereabouts of "Lighthouse" McNeil, he was told that the plane was ready and McNeil had already flown off: "He's probably over Baker Lake by now!"[35] The coach was not pleased.

After acceptance tests, the Norseman was flown to Shediac, New Brunswick on floats and then back to Ontario where all RCMP

35   Baker Lake is located in what is now Nunavut.

The Norseman.

Norseman CF MPE, the first RCMP aircraft in the North, seen here under the low level bridge in Edmonton. McNeil is on the far right.

aircraft were stored for the winter. The following summer the plane was flown on floats on a route that went from Orient Bay, Ontario through Lac du Bonnet, Manitoba to Prince Albert, Saskatchewan, finally landing at Cooking Lake, near Edmonton, Alberta.

McNeil's account of his flight down the Mackenzie River reads like an adventurer's novel:

Flying down the Mackenzie River, we made a brief visit to all detachments en route to Aklavik. The next day, we flew to Fort Norman, Great Bear Lake and overnighted at Eldorado. As the water levels at Cooking Lake and the Saskatchewan River were receding, we then moved our base of operations to Fort McMurray, Fort Smith and later to Yellowknife. We surveyed the barren lands, made a wild game count and checked an Eskimo camp by the Aberdeen Lakes. Because of floating sea ice on the west side of Hudson Bay, we did not try landing at any coastal detachments but returned to the lake where we spent about a week.

McNeil's old friend "Wop" May was no longer flying by 1939. He had lost the sight in one eye and his license had been suspended. But McNeil invited May to join him on a flight in the North. They flew out of Fort Simpson over Herschel Island just as the famed RCMP *St. Roch* was on its epic journey through the Northwest Passage.

We thought we saw St. Roch *in the distance, but there was quite a bit of fog coming in. We saw Herschel Island and Shemel Point and then came back and landed.*

Taking May's advice, they came back down the Mackenzie River, stopping at Fort Providence, Fort Rae, Fort Reliance, Fort Resolution and Fort Smith.

Because war with Germany was imminent, there were suspicions about a priest who was flying some missions. In those scary times, some people thought the priest—who had been in the German Air Force—might be a spy, putting in caches that could be valuable to the Germans should they attack the North. So RCMP members, including McNeil, went around and moved caches of barrels of aviation gas that had been hidden in the Northwest Territories. The suspicions about the priest were apparently unfounded since nothing came of it.

McNeil was flying a mission out of Yellowknife when he heard over the radio that war had been declared against Germany. Having served in the Army reserve earlier in his life, he radioed in to volunteer immediately and received orders to report to Ottawa to initiate his transfer to the Royal Canadian Air Force. The RCMP agreed to allow any members with flying experience to join the military for the duration of the war, assuring them they could return to the RCMP when the war ended. And so McNeil was loaned to the RCAF, along with several other RCMP members who had Air Force experience. The entirety of the RCMP's "Air" Division was soon under the jurisdiction of the RCAF.

MANY YEARS AFTER McNeil's retirement, a long-time friend of McNeil's son Cam, George Dewar, arranged a meeting between McNeil and famed pilot Al Lilly. The two had learned to fly together in Moose Jaw in 1932. Lilly had wanted to join the RCMP "Air" Division with McNeil but was refused permission because the Force had spent money training him as a dog master. Lilly eventually left the Force and became chief test pilot for Canadair. He was the first Canadian to break the sound barrier, flying a Sabre, and was the Canada's answer to famed American test pilot Chuck Yeager. Lilly was also the chief test pilot for Ferry Command during the war and is the only former member of the RCMP in the Canadian Aviation Hall of Fame. Lilly, himself a member of the Order of Canada, said that Stirling McNeil was one of his heroes.

Lilly and McNeil had not seen each other for 60 years, but Dewar said it seemed they had only been apart for a week: "It was remarkable to see two elderly gentlemen with what amounted to total recall, discussing their careers in aviation and the events of their lives."

While Lilly talked of his experiences in Ferry Command, McNeil spoke of the first RCMP flight into the Arctic in a Norseman. Dewar added, "One thing I noticed during the two hours they met was that never once did either brag about anything. When you have accomplished something significant, you don't have to brag about it." McNeil was 93 and Lilly exactly two years younger—they shared the same birthday.[36]

---

36 After that incredible experience, Cam McNeil returned to Ottawa and contacted then-Supt. Greg Peters, Director of the Heritage Branch. The RCMP was not aware of Lilly's incredible career after leaving the Force at the beginning of the war. Supt. Peters, a pilot himself, sent a historian to write Lilly's life story. Lilly died at age 98.

On May 26, 2010, at the RCMP Air Services Hanger in Ottawa, "Hawk One," the Canadian Centennial of Flight F-86 Sabre jet, was named the *Al Lilly*. Supt. Peters spoke of Lilly's life in the Force, including his friendship with Stirling McNeil. Astronaut Colonel Chris Hadfield—the Sabre pilot, accomplished test pilot, *(cont'd)*

AL LILLY WAS not the only member of the Aviation Hall of Fame to share a friendship of mutual admiration with Stirling McNeil. Many of the greats retired to Victoria, joined the Air Force Officers Association and/or the Royal United Services Institute and elected McNeil their president. To them, McNeil was "our Mountie." They knew of his pre-war pioneer flying in the North, his war service with the RCAF as a Wing Commander, and his return to the RCMP as a senior Air Force officer.

Among those who called McNeil a friend were: Lt. Gen. Reg Lane, DSO, DFC, CD—three tours as a bomber and pathfinder pilot who flew the *Ruhr Express*, the first Canadian built Lancaster to England; Mike Cooper-Slipper, DFC, test pilot of the Avro Arrow and its engine, the Iroquois, and the first Jetliner; and "Wop" May, DFC, pioneer bush pilot and World War 1 ace with 13 kills, the man whom the Red Baron was trying to shoot down when he himself was killed; and Grant McConachie, founder and president of Canadian Pacific Airlines.[37]

Another friendship treasured by both Stirling and Carolyn McNeil was the one they shared with Major General the Honourable George Pearkes, VC, PC, CC, CB, DSO, MC, CD,

---

Canada's first Commander of the International Space Station, and member of the Hall of Fame and the Order of Canada—spoke movingly of Lilly's aviation pioneering. It was a great day. The Lilly family, Cam McNeil and Stirling McNeil's great-grandson, Garrett Stirling McNeil, 12, were there to see it.

37 When Cam and his son attended the 50th anniversary of his 436 Squadron, the two guests of honour were Brg. General Ralph Gordon, DSO, DFC, first CO of 436 and the only RCAF transport pilot to earn the DSO, and Col. O.B. Philp, founding father of the Snowbirds. Stirling McNeil had been the class senior of Gordon's flying class, and Cam was Gordon's son Larry's senior in the Dalhousie Squadron. Larry was later senior DC-9 pilot with Air Canada and asked Cam to be a pallbearer at Gordon's funeral. When Cam asked Philp if he knew his dad, Philp burst out laughing: "Stirling calls me his favourite Groupie!" (RCAF slang for Group Captain, now Colonel.)

and Mrs. Pearkes. A winner of the Victoria Cross in the First World War, Gen. Pearkes was perhaps British Columbia's most distinguished soldier. He was very proud of the fact that he had been a Corporal in the Royal North West Mounted Police. When he was Lieutenant-Governor of British Columbia, the couples met and a friendship developed. When Gen. Pearkes died, McNeil arranged for his tombstone. Mrs. Pearkes, who seldom travelled after her husband's death, made a special trip from Vancouver to attend Carolyn and Stirling's 50th wedding anniversary. They were honoured, and deeply touched.

THE LOVE OF HIS LIFE

THE CHANCE MEETING between Carolyn Stauffer and Stirling McNeil at Edmonton's Macdonald Hotel changed their lives.

As he was coming in the revolving door, a beautiful woman was going out. McNeil had seen this woman before when he was in Lethbridge. She was gorgeous and very popular. He thought he would not have a chance with her but he approached her anyway. 'You're Carry Stauffer,' he said. She smiled and said, 'How do I know you?' He introduced himself and soon struck up a conversation. They began to date. At age 31, they were both getting kind of old for those days not to be married.[38]

Miss Stauffer had received many proposals but there was one thing standing in the way of accepting them—her father. Mr. Stauffer had been a member of the North West Mounted Police and had never liked the men his daughter had brought home. That is,

---

38   Regina and District Old Timers' Association, *Keepers of the Law* (Regina, SK: Regina and District Old Timers' Association, 2005).

until Stirling McNeil came along. Partly because he was an RCMP member and probably because Mr. Stauffer saw something special in McNeil, he gave his blessing.[39] However, getting her father's permission was only one obstacle to wedded bliss. RCMP policy at the time required members to have five years' service and $500 in the bank. Mr. Stauffer had encountered the same problem years earlier in the North West Mounted Police. He had had to purchase his discharge from the NWMP in order to get married. Stirling McNeil applied for permission to marry, but there was another hurdle. Prospective wives of members had to be thoroughly investigated by the Force.[40] As their son Cam put it, "They had to make sure she was a woman of high repute and that she would be a suitable Mounted Police wife."

Stirling and Carolyn were finally approved to marry, but more roadblocks would be thrown in their path. Canada was now at war and the RCMP "Air" Division was joining the Royal Canadian Air Force. When Canada declared war on Germany, McNeil was flying a routine mission out of Yellowknife to Baker Lake as a Lance Corporal with the RCMP, but he landed as a probationary Pilot Officer with the Royal Canadian Air Force on his return.[41] Now under Air Force command, he had to apply for permission to marry Carolyn all over again. According to Cam McNeil, "they were the most officially approved couple that ever walked down the aisle."

Their decision to marry was hastened by the war in Europe as it

---

39 Carolyn's father purchased his discharge from the NWMP to marry her mother, who lived in a sod-roof hut near Neudorf, SK. In 1908, they were the first to drive a car from Saskatchewan to Ontario. Stauffer Lake, SK is named for them.

40 Regina and District Old Timers' Association.

41 Pilot Officer was the lowest commissioned rank in the RCAF.

appeared that most of McNeil's classmates would be sent overseas. Carolyn, engagement ring on one hand and wedding ring on the other for safekeeping, went by train on her own from Edmonton to Toronto. McNeil had been stationed in Ontario for additional flight training. Before leaving Alberta, Carolyn had to say goodbye to her father, who was dying of cancer.

McNeil was tied up in flying school and was thus unable to meet his bride at the train station in Toronto. "Don't worry, my brother Campbell is going to come and pick you up," McNeil had written to Carolyn. "And don't worry about who he is. Look for the handsomest man in the train station."

Likewise, McNeil had written to his brother, "Look for the most beautiful woman in the train station and that will be Carolyn."

The Toronto train station was large and, in the midst of the war, crowded. And yet, when Carolyn got off the train and into the station, she and Campbell walked right into each other. Her future husband's brother then took her to the church where the wedding was to take place and arranged for his own sister-in-law to be Carolyn's bridesmaid. He had also arranged for flowers—beautiful orchids.

The bride changed into her wedding clothes, a brown jacket and skirt with a matching fur collar. Then McNeil arrived with all the men who could get a pass for the wedding. And so of those in attendance, Carolyn really knew only one person at her wedding: her husband.

Stirling and Carolyn were married January 6, 1940. They had two children: Cam, born September 11, 1941, and Barbara, born May 3, 1945.

Carolyn and Stirling on their wedding day in Toronto,
January 6, 1940.

The McNeils stayed overnight in Toronto and had their wedding pictures taken the next day by a photographer from a Toronto newspaper. McNeil wore his Air Force uniform instead of red serge. Their honeymoon was delayed for a week because McNeil was a class senior who believed in looking after fellow pilots younger than himself. He was particularly concerned about one young pilot, a teenager who was deeply homesick. And so the McNeils did not go on their honeymoon on their own—they took the lonely young pilot, Dougie Brooker, with them. Brooker, who later married and founded the very successful AERO burner company of Toronto, and his wife were life-long friends of the McNeils.

A PORTRAIT OF Chief Iron Shield, who dealt with the North West Mounted Police in signing Treaty No 7, is now a McNeil family heirloom. The artist, Nicholas de Grandmaison, was known for his portraits of Indigenous people, and had a collection in Regina's Mackenzie Art Gallery and Calgary's Glenbow Museum.

Born in 1892 to a French and Russian family of noble descent, de Grandmaison regarded the Plains First Nations as "the aristocrats of North America and through his romantic vision saw in their weathered features a strength he wished to preserve."[42]

Making his way to England following the war, [de Grandmaison] studied at the St. John's Wood Art School in London…. He immigrated to Canada in 1923 and settled in Banff, Alberta.

42 "de Grandmaison, Nicholas," Loch Gallery, http://www.lochgallery.com/artist/de-grandmaison-nicholas. Accessed March 17, 2016.

"Chief Iron Shield," signer of Treaty 7 with NWMP, given to Stirling McNeil by Nicholas de Grandmaison.

Wishing to discover more about his adopted country, de Grandmaison often travelled from his home in the mountains to the prairies.[43]

He sought the acquaintance of Indigenous people along the way, inspiring a purposeful choice in the subject matter of his portraiture: "'… to me it is a great honour … they have colour, character and history in their blood.'"[44]

But it was when he was living in Calgary that de Grandmaison met McNeil. McNeil received a call that de Grandmaison, having perhaps had "one too many" at the Palliser Hotel, needed assistance getting home. There was, however, a slight problem—the hotel bill still needed to be paid. McNeil dipped into his own pocket to cover the amount, worth about three weeks' pay. In return, the artist gave McNeil a portrait of Chief Iron Shield.

McNeil came home to tell his new wife that instead of the whole month's salary, he had a week's pay and a grand painting. It was a generous gift; the value of Nicholas de Grandmaison's paintings has accrued nicely over the years.

43 "Nicholas de Grandmaison," www.mayberryfineart.com, http://www.mayberry-fine-art.com/artist/nicholas_de_grandmaison. Accessed March 17, 2016.

44 www.mayberryfineart.com.

THE WAR YEARS

When war broke out in 1939, McNeil was a Lance Corporal in the RCMP with eight years' service. He and the rest of "Air" Division were seconded to the RCAF, where he was accepted as a probationary pilot officer.

Wing Commander Donald Macdonald, DFC and Bar,[45] RCAF (Rtd.)—who won his Distinguished Flying Crosses for flying DeHavilland Mosquito planes on night intruder missions to enemy airfields—called McNeil a "gentle giant" whose standards of conduct were much higher than most:

He never tried to dictate what people did, but set an example. He was group leader for pilot officers course No. 5. I was the leader for the last course, No. 6. The would-be pilots in those

45 Distinguished Flying Cross and Bar. "The cross is awarded to officers and Warrant Officers for an act or acts of valour, courage or devotion to duty performed whilst flying in active operations against the enemy .... A straight silver bar is awarded for a further act or acts of valour, courage or devotion to duty whilst flying in active operations against the enemy." Veterans Affairs Canada, http://www.veterans.gc.ca/eng/remembrance/medals-decorations/orders-decorations/dfc. Accessed March 17, 2016.

days were a first-class group, university graduates and students. Stirling called the roll for the group each day and marched them down to the hangars. One day, one of the young bucks gave him some lip. Stirling went up to the young man, lifted him a couple feet off the ground and gently put him back down again. He did not say a word but discipline was established.

Macdonald, then OC RCAF Station Rockcliffe, also remembered Stirling's sense of humour and fun:

When he was in charge of the Musical Ride, he visited Joan and me at our home. It must have been on a weekend, but Stirling was in full dress uniform. I was going to escort him back up to the bus. When we left the house, it was apparent that a lot of the neighbours were outside starting their spring gardening. Stirling grabbed me and put my arm behind my back and told me, in a loud voice, to come quietly and not make a fuss. He marched me around the corner out of sight of the neighbours. There, we both started to laugh.

IN THE RCAF, Stirling was stationed in many different places. At one point, he was head of Air Force Police in Calgary. He was promoted rapidly through the ranks to Flying Officer, Flight Lieutenant, Squadron Leader and then Wing Commander, in charge of Security and Intelligence on the Pacific Coast. In that capacity, he represented the Air Force at a meeting where it was decided that Japanese Canadians would be sent inland and their property seized. It was one of the worst things our government has done to its citizens. But even in those days, when many people feared the Japanese and looked askance at Japanese Canadians, McNeil and the RCMP representative knew that it was the wrong thing to do. "Do not do this," they said. "There is no need. We have had zero incidents of sabotage or sedition or anything else. And besides, these are Canadian citizens."

McNeil protested to no avail and, sadly, Japanese Canadians were forced to move to the B.C. interior and the Prairies. Their properties were literally stolen. It remains a sad chapter in Canada's history. The two groups with the most responsibility had there been any problem with Japanese Canadians were the Air Force, who had installations all along the coast, and the Mounted Police, who were primarily charged with making sure nothing happened. With his firsthand knowledge of both RCAF security and the RCMP, McNeil knew Japanese Canadians were not a threat, yet his wishes were ignored. At the time, he said, "There was no sign of disloyalty. They were good citizens. But the public's mind was made up."

BUT JAPAN'S THREAT to the West Coast *was* very real and the RCAF was on the front line. The Japanese captured two Alaskan islands and a submarine had shelled a Vancouver Island lighthouse. McNeil was responsible for the security of all the secret radar bases, airbases and other RCAF installations on the coast. Inspecting them was not easy. A number could only be reached in good weather by breeches buoy [46] and high line from a boat.

---

46   "A canvas seat in the form of breeches hung from a life buoy running on a *(cont'd)*

One of the vessels that took McNeil on his inspection trips was a US Navy motor gunboat commanded by Robert Young, movie and TV star, best known as the father in *Father Knows Best*. Stirling liked him and agreed that, indeed, father does know best.

Stirling valued his role as husband and father, though he was away a good deal of the time. When he was home, he enjoyed spending time with young Cam, swimming in the sea with him on his back or following Cam's tiny outrigger canoe. Once, Stirling shaved off his mustache for an officer's mess skit and came home to find Cam would not let this "strange man" in the house. It was the last time he shaved off his mustache.

MCNEIL CONTINUED IN the RCAF and competed as part of the RCAF rugby team in the inter-service championship with the Navy. After the game was over, the Air Officer commanding Western Air Command called McNeil over and told him his playing days were over. He didn't want his Director of Security and Intelligence to be flattened by a Navy stoker—it was bad for business!

SEVERAL TIMES IN his career, McNeil came in contact with the legendary skipper Henry Larsen of the RCMP *St. Roch*, renowned for making the first voyage through the Northwest Passage, west to east, in one season, and the first vessel to circumnavigate North America. When *St. Roch* arrived in Vancouver, McNeil, as Air

---

hawser and used to haul persons from one ship to another or from ship to shore especially in rescue operations." Merriam-Webster Dictionary, http://www.merriam-webster.com/dictionary/breeches%20buoy. Accessed March 17, 2016.

Force representative, was on the docks to welcome Larsen. They had known each other in the Arctic. And so it was no surprise that Larsen gave McNeil some artifacts he had found, including a cannon that had been left by the Royal Navy in the early 1800s when they were searching for the Franklin Expedition.[47] McNeil used his Air Force contacts to have the artifacts flown to Regina for display at the RCMP Heritage Centre. Some of McNeil's Arctic gear is also on display there, as is his pilot's logbook.

McNEIL DID EXTREMELY well in the military, and was honoured by being Mentioned in Dispatches for service during the Second World War.[48] As Wing Commander in charge of Security and Intelligence, he travelled all over Western Air Command, often to the secret radar bases along the coast. He had his own airplane, pilot and driver. The Air Force wanted him to remain in the service after the war, offering to reduce his rank by only one step to Squadron Leader even though the custom was to drop two ranks to remain in service during peace time. Because of his police background, McNeil spent much of his military service dealing with intelligence

---

47   Regina and District Old Timers' Association.

"In 1845, explorer Sir John Franklin set sail from England with two ships, HMS Erebus and HMS Terror, in search of a Northwest Passage across what is now Canada's Arctic. The ships and crews vanished, prompting a massive search that continues to this day." HMS Erebus was found in September 2014. Franklin is believed to have died aboard. "The Franklin Expedition," Parks Canada, http://www.pc.gc.ca/eng/culture/franklin/index.aspx. Accessed May 4, 2016.

48   "Mention in Dispatches shall be awarded for valiant conduct, devotion to duty or other distinguished service." Canadian Honours Chart, National Defence and the Canadian Forces, http://www.cmp-cpm.forces.gc.ca/dhr-ddhr/chc-tdh/chart-tableau-eng.asp?ref=MiD. Accessed March 17, 2016.

Wing Commander Stirling McNeil MiD, Vancouver, B.C. (McNeil gave this hat to his Cam when his son was commissioned. Cam still wears it on Remembrance Day.)

and security, and never got the opportunity to go overseas in combat. While that had pleased his wife, McNeil always regretted that he had never gone to the European theatre of war.

Throughout their marriage the McNeils kept a guest book, the first two pages of which were signed by McNeil's classmates from flying school. Two died during the Battle of Britain.

If McNeil had had any inclination to stay in the RCAF, he was firmly discouraged by Commr. S. T. Wood, who had always been reluctant to send his men off to war because there was a tremendous workload to be shouldered by police in wartime. The Commissioner was said to have been annoyed that his "Marine" Division had gone to the Navy and the "Air" Division to the Air Force during the war.

RCMP MEMBERS HAD been promised that they would keep their rank when they came back to the Force, but during the six years over which the Second World War unfolded, anyone who was a good policeman in the RCMP had been promoted two or three times. Even outstanding officers like L.H. Nicholson, OC Number 1 Provost Company in the Army returned to the RCMP with the same rank he had held before the war—Inspector. Nicholson quickly advanced through the post-war ranks of the RCMP to become Commissioner, and McNeil was commissioned in Nicholson's first promotion list. Many say Nicholson, a man of principle, was the best Commissioner the Force ever had, and McNeil followed him back to the RCMP. McNeil, who, according to the RCMP, had had "a good war," was immediately promoted to the RCMP rank of Corporal.

ON TO THE PRAIRIES

BACK IN THE RCMP, Cpl. McNeil and his wife Carolyn were headed to a small detachment in rural Saskatchewan. Before leaving Vancouver, the Air Force officers fêted them.

The McNeils took the train to Saskatoon, where they were stationed for a short time, then it was off to the tiny village of Young—where they had to buy water for the princely sum of $5 a barrel because the local water was stagnant and alkaline. It wasn't quite what the former Wing Commander and his wife were used to. With an adventuresome spirit, they soon adjusted to the new lifestyle.

In many one-man detachments, the work was often shared by the RCMP member's spouse—especially when the detachment office also served as living quarters. So it was for the McNeils, and Carolyn became the detachment's "second man."

There were no police radios in RCMP vehicles back then so when Cpl. McNeil went on patrol, there was no way to contact him. One night, a man—wildly drunk and covered in blood—came to the detachment to report he had been assaulted. Diminutive

Carolyn McNeil invited him in and cleaned the blood from his face. "Come this way, sir," she said, gently leading him into the office and make-shift jail cell. She told him he would be comfortable there and locked him in. Wives of many RCMP members in small detachments had similar stories of pitching in when their husbands were not available.

Wives also had occasion to ride in the police car with their husbands. Cst. Mullen Hughes (Reg. No. 12947) wrote of an encounter with an intoxicated female he arrested for displaying her wares on a busy highway, distracting truckers and nearly causing an accident. Hughes had no choice but to arrest the woman and take her to the cells. With the prisoner in the back seat and his wife Theresa beside him, Hughes began the return trip to the detachment. But he had forgotten about an empty, one-gallon glass jug on the floor of the police car, near the back seat.

All of a sudden, the prisoner whacked the policeman's wife on the side of the head with the glass jug. Hughes braked hard, throwing the woman forward into the front seat and pushing his wife under the dash. The prisoner then tried to grab Theresa's hair. Hughes ended the fracas with a blow to the prisoner's head. The policeman's wife later said she felt dizzy but was fortunate to not have any serious injury. Just another day of married life in the RCMP.[49]

Stirling McNeil's career progressed in Saskatchewan, and he was promoted to Sergeant and transferred to the larger community of Biggar, where he was in charge of a three-man detachment.

---

49 Don Saul, ed.

ACCORDING TO SUPT. Don Duke (Rtd.), one of the responsibilities of detachment commanders was to check on the local graves of deceased members, and Sgt. McNeil was no exception. He checked on the grave of deceased member Ernie Meakings in Biggar and found the grave to be in good order.

A highway sign outside the town of Biggar proclaims, "New York is big—but this is Biggar." Apparently, Carolyn McNeil thought the novelty of the sign might appeal to a national magazine. She was right, and won $5 for submitting the item to *Reader's Digest*. Cam McNeil joked that when he was young he lived in Young and when he got bigger he moved to Biggar.

Bob Brownlee was a young man living in Biggar in 1946:

Sgt. McNeil got a lot of us kids involved in helping to dig the first swimming pool. He would sometimes go out and clean out the town's two beer parlours if he needed a little extra help.

Brownlee added that one guy told him that he and a few of his friends had been paid a small amount of money for their work. But they didn't keep it very long: "Sgt. McNeil would come around and say, 'Thanks for the donation, boys,' and put the money in the fund for building the pool."

Brownlee himself joined the RCMP in 1949 and was posted to Edmonton the following year. By then, McNeil had been promoted to Sergeant Major, the top NCO in "K" Division.[50] Brownlee recalled that although McNeil "was the guy who did the disciplining," he was also "a real likeable guy—gung-ho."

---

50   Alberta.

Sgt. Major Stirling McNeil,
Edmonton, AB

Commissioner Robert H. Simmonds, Order of Canada, remembered his first day at "K" Division headquarters.[51] He arrived in his own car on a cold winter day and, having left the car running, went in to find out where to go. When he returned, the car was locked and the keys were gone. He went back to the desk to be told the Sergeant Major wanted to see him. McNeil welcomed him to "K" Division with a lecture so effective that he never in his life left the keys in a car again.

Life in Edmonton was memorable for the McNeil children. McNeil's daughter Barbara remembers the barracks square well:

> *It was still standing the last time I was in Edmonton.... We [lived] in a house, a triplex that had the Sergeant Major on the left as you faced the house and two Staff Sergeants [on the right]. Further to the left were the old stables, which were then used for storage and as a garage. We used to play in those stables.*

McNeil continued to participate in sports—it seemed he excelled at everything from football to tennis; he would play matches against young constables and run them into the ground. McNeil was close to the Edmonton Eskimos football team and met such football notables as manager Al Anderson, Coach Annis Stukus, Normie Kwong,[52] Jackie Parker, Rollie Prather, and many other

---

51 The RCMP was not Comm. Simmonds first career choice. As a teen in the Second World War, he wanted to fly naval Spitfires for the Royal Navy. He rode his bicycle 90 miles from his farm to Saskatoon for his medical. The war ended before his training. No Spitfire, no job, thus the RCMP. He was Commissioner for 10 years, the longest in the modern era. In 2014, Cam McNeil helped him into his first Spitfire cockpit. He has "every book on Spitfires."

52 Later to become Lieutenant Governor of Alberta.

players. The McNeils even hosted a few of them for dinner on occasion. Out of town players really appreciated the gesture.

And McNeil's continued involvement in sports must have kept him in good shape. After a traffic accident he attended, his formidable strength allowed him to lift a car off a man.

Although often involved in community and sports activities, McNeil was a policeman 24 hours a day. He always carried a ticket book. He might be driving with the family in the car, but if he saw a traffic violation, he would take off in a flurry of gravel to catch the offender. Even in civilian clothes, he would stop the car and give the driver a lecture and a warning ticket. And if you were on the receiving end of a lecture from Stirling McNeil, you *knew* he had authority! He had a presence about him and expected to be obeyed. He was always on duty.[53]

The family's next move on the Prairies was to Regina in 1951, where McNeil was appointed Adjutant, then Training Officer at "Depot." The family was temporarily put up in the Hotel Saskatchewan until their living quarters were ready. It was Christmas time and the hotel had a huge Christmas tree in the dining room. Barbara recalled, "It must have been 18 feet tall, but it was *my* tree because I was the only little kid besides my brother in the hotel." The McNeils stayed at Hotel Saskatchewan until they could get into "Poverty Row," the

---

53 S/Sgt. Dave Holmes (Rtd.) recalled that even when McNeil was a Superintendent, he carried his ticket book and did not hesitate to write up any infraction he witnessed. One of his pet peeves was the number of "joy riding" complaints. He would read the daily log, and whenever he saw this type of complaint he would question if the complainant had left the keys in the ignition. If that were the case, he would personally phone to chastise the car owner!

nickname given a group of five houses at "Depot" where junior officers lived. Barbara joked that it was poverty for their family because new officers were required to purchase all their kit, which included a ceremonial sword, silver scabbard, and a beautiful, heavy, gold-thread knotted sword belt, replete with hanging tassels. McNeil also had an officer's tunic, officer's shirt, mess kit, and a cape that went over the mess kit. Most newly commissioned officers didn't have to buy the whole kit all at once; they could borrow an item from other officers when needed. But S/Insp. McNeil was now on the training base and had to have it all because there were so many formal functions he was expected to attend. In the McNeil household, the majority of the closet space was dedicated not to Carolyn McNeil's things but rather to Stirling's uniforms and various regalia.

It wasn't always easy being a Mountie's child and Barbara was still quite small when the family moved to Regina:

> *I just remember [my father's] blue pants and yellow stripe. I would trot beside him as he marched on the barracks square and I had to run to keep up. Those were the days when it was not seemly to pick up your child and carry them, or even hold their hand when in uniform.*

There were other constraints to living in barracks. Bicycles could never be left on the front lawn and children had to always be respectful and polite. One of the schools Barbara attended was not highly regarded. Her father became president of the Parent Teacher Association and ensured that they put hot water in the school. He also made sure the asphalt playground had a fence around it because there was traffic on all sides. McNeil was a strong supporter of schools and community activities wherever he was posted.

YOUNG CAM McNEIL was well liked at "Depot," and members thought he was a great kid when he served as bat boy for the baseball team. Cpl. Jack Thornton (Rtd.)[54] recalled being a "barrack brat" with Cam; they used to crawl down through the underground heating systems.

We used to go out and ride the horses and the recruits hated us because while we got to ride the horses, they were the ones who had to saddle [them] up ... for practice and do the work. All we did was ride them.

---

54   Thornton followed in his father's footsteps as a member of the RCMP and was well known in "E" Division, where he earned the nickname "Kodak Jack" for his habit of taking pictures. He was a fixture at B.C. Lions facilities, often using his own vehicle to transport players to and from the airport. Thornton sometimes also drove then-retired Supt. McNeil to a number of functions when McNeil moved to Langley:

He couldn't drive, so for dinners in Abbotsford at the Rancho Hall, I would phone and pick him up and take him out there. He would always be acknowledged by the crowd attending. Everyone would recognize him.

Recalling his family days at "Depot," Thornton added, "Stirling was the Adjutant. I just called him, 'sir.' He was Stirling in name and in nature."

Thornton's father Charles was highly respected by McNeil. Years after his retirement in 1988, McNeil wrote:

I was happy to note that my old colleague Chas. E. Thornton is still going strong at veterans' annual dinners. He was my 'DI' Corporal and room monitor when I was a recruit. When I was posted to 'Depot' as Adjutant, I was pleased to have him as an efficient Sergeant Major.

While Jack Thornton wasn't aware that the officer's houses were known as "poverty row," he did recall that the officers lived in the houses on the north side of the parade square and his family lived on the south side, where senior NCOs like his father were quartered.

In front of the McNeil house, #8 Barracks Square, was the oldest tree in Regina, a cottonwood brought by NWMP dispatch riders in saddlebags as a seedling from the Qu'Appelle Valley to the bald plains that later became the green city of Regina. "It was a real monster—a cottonwood," recalled Cam. The houses had been brought in by rail from Ontario as prefabs in about 1885, set up and bricked on the sides. On the east side of the square were three houses in a complex known as "Brass Row"—the homes of "F" Division's Commanding Officer, "Depot" Division's Commanding Officer, and another senior officer. The tree and houses are no longer there.

McNeil's children have fond memories of Regina. Cam recalled:

I used to go rafting on Wascana Creek, ride the Mounted Police horses, shoot targets on the ranges, swim in the pool and play in the gym. It was pure gold for a kid—just great.

Cam remembered a particular meal at home in Regina, one cooked by two Pakistani princes. As senior police officers studying at the Canadian Police College, they had been away from home for many months, and were lonely and missing their native dishes. Carolyn invited them to dinner and asked if they had recipes that she could prepare.

"Oh no!" they said. They were excellent cooks and would bring everything and prepare the meal themselves. It was a disaster.

The princes thought they could cook but had servants who did all the real food preparation. Everyone had a good laugh and ate leftovers. When the princes returned home, they sent the McNeil children a wonderful badminton set.

Years later, when the Officer Commanding "Depot" visited Pakistan as part of a high level delegation, the group was met by a splendid mounted escort and carriage, as well as a bus. The ranking general moved toward the carriage, but was politely ushered to the bus. The carriage was for the RCMP.

The princes had not forgotten.

FRED RHODES, A young recruit in 1952, still remembers what he called "the shrill voice" of Insp. McNeil:

We were all on parade there in Regina, down by the old 'C' Block, and you could hear this shrill voice coming through the morning mist, calling us to attention. It would kind of wake us up as it was the first parade of the day. This shrill voice came through the atmosphere and we were the young troop at the back. We thought, 'Who the heck was that?' We hadn't heard it before.

Rhodes and other recruits soon got to know the routine: tend to the horses in the morning and go for a run in Regina, come back and have breakfast and queue up for parade. The morning parade consisted of six troops, each with 32 members, for a total of 192 recruits. Rhodes never got to know Insp. McNeil personally but knew everyone respected him.

Cam also recalls his dad in action. It's clear McNeil had a very loud voice:

I would run to school and I would have to be on the other side of the footbridge across Wascana Creek, which was a mile away from the parade square, when I heard my dad yell, 'Parade, Attention!' and if I wasn't on the other side I would be late for school. You could set your watch by him.[55]

STIRLING McNEIL WAS seconded twice while in Regina. Once to serve as the Canadian representative to the US Navy Task Force that was building the Distant Early Warning Line (DEW Line) of radar stations in the eastern Arctic. The US Navy had asked for a Canadian Rear Admiral, but Canada replied that all three admirals were busy and sent RCMP Officer McNeil instead.

The Yankees said, "Great—have him bring his red suit."

For McNeil, it was a return to the Arctic where he had a wonderful adventure. He was aboard the flagship of the task force, *USS Tanner*, a hydrographic vessel. McNeil's colour slides from the trip were wonderful: polar bears, icebergs, rugged mountains, Inuit and ships. He had always loved the North.

Later, he said that he went to the high Arctic as part of the task force "to make sure they didn't decimate the animals" and to ensure that the US Navy respected Canadian law. At Frobisher Bay, RCMP members had to act as postmaster, handling the many bags of mail that came in for the construction crews.

55 Regina and District Old Timers' Association.

*Our fellows, on their time off, were busy sorting mail. People
would come in and say, 'Anything for John Smith?' Someone else
would ask if there was mail for the company, and so on.*

McNeil put in a strong report about the Frobisher Bay detachment being saddled with the work of the postmaster. Some people would come off a ship in the middle of the night and expect to get their mail. He suggested that, at least on a temporary basis, some provision be made to start a post office and have somebody do the job. In those days, the Force did everything. "If something was lost, we'd find it. If people couldn't fix something, they came down to the police. They looked to the Force for everything."

McNeil was also ordered to be ready to command an RCMP Force for peacekeeping duties in Cyprus, which would have been a first both for the RCMP and for Canada. However, that plan was changed and the Army was sent in when shooting escalated.

McNeil's second secondment while serving in Regina was a memorable assignment—he became the Officer in Command of the Musical Ride.

McNeil and his family were very happy in Regina. In fact, of all their homes, Cam said "it was the most special. That is why both [my] parents are buried in the cemetery there."

THE MUSICAL RIDE

In 1952, Insp. McNeil was appointed Officer in Command of the Musical Ride, responsible for conducting the Ride's first tour to the United States since the war.[56] It was to be a remarkable tour.

Riding Master S/Sgt. Ralph Cave—described by one officer as probably the best horseman the Force ever had—recalled an image of McNeil in the saddle. "He was a very tall man and very well turned out." The Ride went to Los Angeles and San Francisco.

You can imagine the impact McNeil would have had on those Hollywood girls. He was a big, tall man in red serge on a magnificent black horse about 16 hands high.

---

56 "The RCMP Musical Ride is performed by a full troop of 32 riders and their horses. Their performance consists of intricate figures and drills choreographed to music. These movements demand the utmost control, timing and coordination. The Musical Ride performs in up to 50 communities across Canada between the months of May and October. They help raise thousands of dollars for local charities and non-profit organizations. The Musical Ride provides the opportunity to experience the heritage and traditions of the RCMP. The riders act as ambassadors of goodwill who promote the RCMP's image throughout Canada and all over the world." "The Musical Ride," Royal Canadian Mounted Police, http://www.rcmp-grc.gc.ca/en/musical-ride. Accessed May 4, 2016.

Some said McNeil had "Clark Gable good looks," complete with a black moustache. In any case, it was obvious the Musical Ride and McNeil personally were big hits in Hollywood. McNeil's daughter Barbara says many Hollywood celebrities—including Susan Hayward, Alan Ladd, and Lucille Ball, Desi Arnaz and their children—loved the Ride. McNeil must have done some little favour for Charlton Heston because they became good friends and exchanged Christmas cards for many years. It may have been that Heston, later head of the National Rifle Association, enjoyed receiving an RCMP-crested Christmas card. Publicity photos of McNeil with Lucille Ball and her children were taken, but they have unfortunately since been lost.

The Ride's visit was the highlight of the Pacific Coast Horse Show Season and received the greatest ovation of any group in California. Perhaps one of the most complimentary things was that many hard-bitten old trainers, usually unimpressed by exhibitors, were seen to return ringside night after night to watch the Mounties perform.

The RCMP can be justly proud of the performance they gave and of the wonderful impression made on the spectators. The sight of 32 scarlet-uniformed riders and their black mounts entering the arena never failed to bring loud cheers from the crowds at each of the 28 performances given in California.

As word spread that the RCMP were in town, more and more people turned out to see the show, some driving as far as 100 miles to see a single performance.[57] Both Los Angeles and San Francisco drew full houses, and many performances were standing room only.

Before and after each performance, the stables were crowded with adoring fans of all ages, and each seemed to be collecting autographs. Fans noted the Mounties were extremely gracious and took time to lead the horses out to be petted, pose for photos with children and answer innumerable questions. Visitors noted that the horses were treated with exceptional kindness and each seemed to be a special pet. At one performance, a drunken man came out of the crowd and pulled a Mountie off his mount. Though riderless, the horse continued doing the routine flawlessly. A famous Hollywood producer suggested to Stirling that they leave that in the act![58]

As OIC, McNeil did not actually take part in the various components of the Ride. According to Riding Master Cave, Insp. McNeil's role was to lead the Ride into the arena and salute the leading dignitary, requesting "permission" for the Ride to proceed. It was a formality, part of tradition.

> *The officer always led the troops in sections [of] four horses. He would give 'troop to the left' or 'troop to the right' wherever the saluting box was and then he would ride up and say a few words and ask for permission to commence the Ride. He would then go off to the side until the 'charge'—the final act of the Ride. McNeil would then lead the Ride off to the music of the RCMP March. When it was over, the men and their steeds broke off and*

---

57   Evelyn Hill.
58   He did not.

went to the railings to give the public a chance to speak to the
riders and pet the horses.[59]

While the Musical Ride was on tour, McNeil's wife and children were left home in Regina. McNeil was away for eight months. This was one of two occasions when Carolyn McNeil was left on her own to shovel snow in Regina, or deal with mosquitoes and muskeg in Northern postings. McNeil also took the Musical Ride to the Royal Winter Fair in Toronto, where Carolyn was able to join him.

---

59   Cave enjoyed working for McNeil. When Cave wanted to wed his fiancée Peggy, he had to seek permission from "headquarters," submitting his application through McNeil, his Commanding Officer. This was during the time of McCarthyism when everyone was worried about communism. Cave's future wife's background had to be checked before permission would be granted. In addition, Cave had to have $500 in the bank. McNeil pretended the permission had not come through right up to the day before they got married.

Later in his career, "Ralph was riding 'Burmese' when the Force presented her to the Queen during the Musical Ride tour of 1969. It was Ralph's original suggestion that the Force should present a horse to the Queen." Supt. Ric Hall (Rtd.), "Your Spurs, Sir!" Royal Canadian Mounted Police Veterans' Association: Vancouver Division—Maintaining the Esprit de Corps. May 28, 2015. http://www.rcmpveteransvancouver.com/your-spurs-sir/. Accessed March 21, 2016.

Cave was one of the 18 members of the B.C. Provincial Police who became part of the Surrey Detachment of the RCMP when they took over policing in 1951. Cave was one of the first to use unmarked police cars for traffic enforcement. For his initiative, he was reprimanded by an officer who said the RCMP would never use such practices to catch speeders. Ralph Cave died on October 12, 2010, at age 85. In *Surrey Now*, Tom Zyratuk said, "Community pillar Ralph Cave wore many hats in Surrey," *Surrey Now*, October 26, 2010, A06. https://issuu.com/canwestcommunitypublishing/docs/srytue20101026. Accessed March 21, 2016).

"PEACE" TIME

ON THE 1ST of November, 1955, Insp. McNeil was posted as Officer Commanding Peace River Sub-Division.[60] The family trip by car from Regina to the town of Peace River was memorable. In North Battleford, the kids were taught the song "The Yellow Rose of Texas" by the OC there, Insp. McComb, who froze to death in a blizzard shortly afterwards. In Whitecourt, northwest of Edmonton, a new road had just pushed through to Valleyview, the Whitecourt cutoff. One section of the new road was so bad that the McNeil car had to be hitched to a bulldozer and skidded through the gumbo.

In his annual report to the Alberta government in 1956, McNeil asked that land be reserved for an RCMP detachment at the junction of the Mackenzie Highway and the Fort Vermillion road as this was an area of oil and other development. The government agreed and sent surveyors to lay out a townsite. Thus McNeil and the RCMP can be credited with helping to found the bustling city of High Level, Alberta—in keeping with the Force's proud tradition as the founders of Calgary, Fort MacLeod, and Fort Steele.

---

60   The northern third of Alberta.

S/Sgt. Joe Naaykens (Rtd.) told a story about McNeil's community activities, which were very similar to what he had done in Biggar, Saskatchewan: he organized local citizens to dig a swimming pool. McNeil was a great public relations man who would greet people on the street, shake hands or give people a friendly signal of thumb and finger to indicate things were OK. One of his "ident" men drew a cartoon of a man wearing a Stetson, emerging from a swimming pool while giving the same kind of OK salute, which was pinned up on a wall in the sub-division office. McNeil didn't mind.

Some members grumbled that McNeil was perhaps more supportive of the public than his own men but that might have been related to the fisticuffs that members sometimes had to engage in. Peace River was a rustic town with loggers, fishermen, oil workers and others filling the bars. "Sometimes," Naaykens said, "Insp. McNeil took his men to task over those incidents."

To keep the peace, McNeil practised what he preached. Even with his family in the car, McNeil would not hesitate to get involved in anything that was happening. On one occasion in downtown Peace River, McNeil singlehandedly broke up a street fight between two men. He grabbed each of them by the scruff of the neck, banged their heads together and ended the fight. Then he carted the miscreants off to jail, putting them in his own car with his family. The CO "K" Division,[61] A/Commr. G.B. McClellan, heard about it and told McNeil that commissioned officers have men to do the rough stuff and not to do something like that again, but that he should maybe run for mayor on the basis of the good publicity.

---

61 Alberta.

Sgt. Dick McLaren (Rtd.) was fresh out of training when he was sent to Peace River, where Insp. McNeil was the OC. McLaren was paid $32 every two weeks. He described McNeil as a "very tall, very good looking, strong-faced, strong-willed person. He was a very personable individual. He ran a very good ship." McLaren and other members had a great deal of respect for Insp. McNeil and would see him from time to time in the sub-division office.

McLaren described the building that served as sub-division headquarters.

It was pretty old. An old, old building that was added on to and restored over the years. We had little cubbyholes for offices and a cell block underneath.

Insp. McNeil had an office adjacent to the RCMP facility and his house was right behind the office. Carolyn McNeil's skill as a hostess was so well known that when Lt. General Guy Simons, Chief of the General Staff and Canada's most famous fighting general of the Second World War, came to town to speak, the McNeils were asked to entertain him.

THE MCNEILS HAD to leave Peace River in a hurry. Barbara recalled that her father was given very short notice that he had been transferred to command "L" Division.[62] It was a very busy time when plans were being made for a Royal Visit, and communication about the transfer was held up somewhere along the way. It

---

62   Prince Edward Island.

came as a complete surprise to McNeil, who had to meet with the Commissioner, who was leaving for a conference in Europe and was on a tight schedule. The family had been in Peace River for four years and now had just four days to pack up and leave.

> *The entire town of Peace River turned out in [a farewell] tribute to him. Within those four days, the mayor, the town council— everybody—had a huge, huge dinner and reception for Mom and Dad the night before we left.*[63]

McNeil had just bought a new car, too, Barbara recalled.

> *The thing went on for miles and miles and was actually Dad's first new car—a Pontiac Safari station wagon—the biggest thing you ever saw in your life. And that's what we drove to Prince Edward Island.*

The island province was still a very quaint place in 1959. The road signs were actually carriage signs designed for the horse and buggy era. The family had a cleaning lady on Prince Edward Island who said the Island was ruined as soon as cars were allowed on it.[64]

---

63 The good people of Peace River presented McNeil with a Styrofoam map of P.E.I. with a plastic mounted policeman on top amongst all kinds of flowers. The floral tribute would have been of special interest to Carolyn McNeil, who had been a commercial florist. In 1939, Carolyn was hired by the Province of Alberta to do all the floral arrangements for the Royal Visit of King George and Queen Elizabeth. The Queen's favourite flower was a white rose and Carolyn had arranged huge masses of that flower for the woman who would be known as the Queen Mother after her daughter Elizabeth II ascended to the Throne.

64 What the cleaning lady would have thought of Confederation Bridge, which now links P.E.I. to the mainland, doesn't bear thinking of.

WELCOME TO P.E.I.

AFTER NO FEWER than 31 postings in 28 years, Stirling McNeil and his wife Carolyn were finally allowed to settle down in one place. In 1959, he was given command of "L" Division, the province of Prince Edward Island. It was to be the final posting of an outstanding career for Stirling McNeil.[65]

The McNeil family soon learned Prince Edward Island was somewhat divided. There were two sides to both politics and religion: Protestant or Catholic; Liberal or Conservative. And the locals had a subtle way of finding out which side you were on. For a short time, the family stayed at a hotel until they could get into their house. They ate their meals in the hotel restaurant. Barbara recalled: "I remember the waitresses being very charming and quite solicitous. They kept asking what school we would go to. When we

---

65 The posting would normally have lasted four years, but the people of P.E.I. loved their "Inspector" McNeil, as they called him. When he became the CO "L" Division, the RCMP classified the position at the rank of Inspector, and he was the only commissioned officer in the province. Two years later, the RCMP re-classified the position at the rank of Superintendent (which most local people were unaccustomed to) and the majority of the population, including the media, continued to affectionately call him "Inspector." McNeil never objected to this understatement of his rank.

said Queen Charlotte, they would nod." This question was intended to determine if the McNeils were Catholic or Protestant. Queen Charlotte Intermediate School was Protestant, so the locals made a judgment accordingly. But McNeil never gave any indication of his religious or political viewpoints, and neither did his family. McNeil had to deal with whatever government was in power and maintained neutrality. His daughter Barbara recalled:

Dad did a good job of that. We always said he would put his own grandmother in jail if she deserved it. He was absolutely honest—incorruptible—and totally impartial.

McNeil's men always appreciated the fact that he always backed them up, provided they were doing their jobs. A senior government official was once picked up for suspected impaired driving. The official told the young policeman who arrested him, "You don't know who I am. I am a government minister and I live across the street from Supt. McNeil."

McNeil got a call from the young policeman, who was likely quaking in his boots. What should he do?

The Superintendent didn't hesitate. "Ah. All right. That's fine. Allow him to call his lawyer. He's in the clink. Hold him there until his lawyer comes."

The official was hot under the collar for a few days, and then realized he had been treated like everyone else—with courtesy. That's exactly how McNeil operated and what he expected of his officers. It didn't matter who you were, you were treated the same way.

On another occasion, McNeil answered a knock on the door to

find the premier wanting to chat. It was the day before the provincial election. Not knowing what the visit was all about, Carolyn commented, "How kind of him to drop by the day before the election—we haven't even been here long enough to be on the Voters' List."

Barbara and her mother sat in the kitchen, thinking the visit must have to do with something official. A few minutes later they heard the man leave.

It was only years later that Supt. McNeil revealed that the premier had dropped by to see if McNeil would instruct the RCMP not to enforce the *Liquor Act* on election day. The premier was perhaps hoping to be able to offer free drinks to supporters.

But McNeil told him, "Of course, the *Liquor Act* will be enforced. It's the law of this Island. Thank you very much for coming and goodbye, sir."

And so it became known that McNeil was straight as an arrow, a nice guy and incorruptible. And, as it turned out, that particular premier was defeated. Supt. McNeil had a unique method of dealing with anyone who improperly asked for a favour. On one occasion he is said to have told an official who was trying to get his friends out of trouble, "Sir, you are my civilian superior. If you give it to me in writing, I will act on it immediately." And that was the end of the matter.

Two problems faced McNeil when he assumed command of "L" Division. One was a situation in Alberton, "up west," as the locals said, in the northwestern part of Prince Edward Island where there were disputes with local fishermen. Some Fisheries Department officers and an RCMP officer had been assaulted. The other problem was the number of traffic fatalities that involved excessive speed and alcohol.

To solve the problem with the tough fishermen, McNeil called in his senior NCO and asked him to identify his toughest and biggest men. Those chosen were transferred immediately to Alberton. McNeil's instructions to the NCO were clear: "Tell the members they are not to refuse a fight." In short order, likely after a skirmish or two, the problem was solved.

Regarding the traffic fatalities, Supt. McNeil wanted "a full court press"—a real push on traffic enforcement with zero tolerance for offenders. He asked about the car and driver that had been assigned to him.

"Yes, sir," said his senior NCO, "as CO, you are entitled to that."

McNeil replied, "I don't need the car or the driver. I'll drive my own car. Assign them both to highway patrol immediately."

McNeil ordered zero tolerance for violations and within a year there were no traffic fatalities on Prince Edward Island.

ONE OF MCNEIL's successors, A/Commr. Ralph Culligan (Rtd.), who served as CO "L" Division from mid-1981 to early 1985, told this story. During McNeil's time, the "L" Division HQ building had limited visitor parking at the front but lots of parking in the rear. There was a reserved space for the CO in the rear parking lot.

One summer Sunday, Supt. and Mrs. McNeil had been out in their family car when Stirling stopped in at the office, parking in one of the front-lot visitors' slots, leaving Mrs. McNeil in the

Fifth annual Charlottetown RCMP Church Parade, 1964, postcard.
Salute taken by the Lieutenant Governor and premier.

car to await his return. He went in, did whatever he had planned to do, but on leaving, absentmindedly exited the HQ building by the back door, got into his Force-equipped vehicle and drove off. Mrs. McNeil, meanwhile, waited patiently for her spouse's return. Culligan remembered, "I believe the wait was in the three-hour range before it was discovered that McNeil was no longer on site and had left his wife behind!"[66]

McNEIL BELIEVED IN the value of tradition and ceremony and used it to raise the popularity of the Force with Islanders. In "Depot," he had seen the positive effects of formal church parades.

---

66   During his time on the Island, Culligan was continually asked if he had ever met Stirling McNeil, or "Mr. P.E.I.," as many called him. Culligan said McNeil was highly recognized by the movers and shakers in P.E.I. Culligan said he did have the good fortune to meet McNeil and was an occasional visitor to his home on Vancouver Island during McNeil's retirement.

Leading the Charlottetown RCMP Church Parade.

Charlottetown RCMP Church Parade postcard.

In Charlottetown, he instituted parades to major churches through downtown in red serge. Charlottetown loved it. Twenty years after the McNeils left, "Mounties Parading to Church" postcards were still best-sellers.

THE MCNEIL CHARM

THOUGH HE WAS from "away," few people charmed the good citizens of Prince Edward Island the way Stirling McNeil did. He became a significant part of the social fabric of Charlottetown.

S/Sgt. Bill Stephens (Rtd.) told the story of a forest fire "up west" in the Alberton area of Prince Edward Island. Volunteer firefighters needed military assistance to fight the fire. RCMP officers also attended, headed by Supt. McNeil.

Supt. McNeil befriended a whole bunch of people, chatting with them after they got the fire out. He made such an impression that people from that area would stop in to see him whenever they came to Charlottetown.

And McNeil remembered their names.

McNeil had a way of solving problems tactfully. Stephens recalled one incident when a citizen came into the office to complain about something. The man was hard of hearing, and the officer at the front counter had to almost shout in order to be heard. The sound of loud voices caused the Superintendent to come out of his office to see what all the shouting was about. Supt. McNeil then took the man into his office, sat him down and listened to his complaint. He must have resolved the matter because the man emerged from McNeil's office "ecstatic" and impressed that he had spoken to the Commanding Officer.

RETIRED A/COMMR. HOWARD "Hap" Armstrong [67] said the following was his favourite story about McNeil:

> Stirling would visit the hospital almost every day and walk into the rooms to say hello to everyone in the room by name. He would ask them how they were doing and if there was anything he could do for them. If there was a request, Stirling would do it. What always amazed the patients was his ability to remember their names each and every time. They talked about it all over the Island. The truth was that Stirling would check with the nurses and get everyone's name, what bed they were in, etc., and in he went. This secret between Stirling and the nurses lasted until long after he was gone.

IT WAS MCNEIL's habit to go for a walk in Charlottetown when he went to the post office to pick up mail for the division. The walkabout would take half the morning because he would stop and talk to nearly everyone he met on the street.

---

67   Another CO "L" Division.

A/Commr. Cort MacDonnell (Rtd.) said McNeil was the epitome of the ultimate gentleman.

I recall a tale of him standing on the street corner in britches and boots—which were the uniform of the day—assisting an elderly lady across the intersection, only to find that she was a little hard of hearing and had not been telling him she wanted to cross the street. Nonetheless, he helped the woman along her way.

Supt. Greg Peters (Rtd.) hailed from the small town of Souris, P.E.I., and considered McNeil's widespread acceptance as remarkable. In Prince Edward Island, an obituary might say, "Boston woman dies in Summerside" and go on to add that the deceased came to the Island as a two-year-old. The converse would be "Island woman dies in Boston." But Stirling McNeil could probably have called himself an Islander because he left a lasting legacy there. At one point, McNeil was nominated for "Islander of the Year" but declined, saying, "That's awfully good of you, but I've just come to the Island. You should give that honour to someone born here," once again endearing himself to the community.

STIRLING AND CAROLYN McNeil fit in perfectly with Charlottetown society. Mrs. McNeil was described by many as a gracious, dignified lady who was very good at entertaining. Her knowledge and experience served the people well when preparations were made for the Royal Visit in 1964. Locals knew that Government House was not quite up to standard, but Carolyn took over and soon had

Stirling McNeil, *HMY Britannia,*
1964

the mansion in fit shape to entertain royalty. She was asked to escort Madame Pauline Vanier, wife of the Governor General, and Mrs. Maryon Pearson, wife of Prime Minister Lester Pearson. Mrs. Pearson is said to have told Carolyn that "behind every good man is a surprised woman." Supt. and Mrs. McNeil spent several minutes talking to the Queen and Prince Philip at the royal dinner, and the McNeils were taken aboard the royal yacht *Britannia.* Their host was the captain, the only Royal Navy Admiral commanding only one ship.

TOWARD THE END of his career, Supt. McNeil was asked by the premier to accept the position of lieutenant governor. He declined because he knew he could not meet the financial demands of that high office on his RCMP pension. In those days, the pension was based on a member's salary on his last day of service. This was subsequently changed to base the pension on the last five years of service. It is doubtful that McNeil ever made more than $20,000 a year.

McNeil was to say years later that his pension cheques over 35 years exceeded the value of his 35 years of paycheques, something that likely "tickled the parsimonious Scot in him."[68] McNeil commented, "I don't mind a bit taking a chunk out of Treasury Board."

---

68   David Guy.

MCNEIL'S "BOYS"

THROUGHOUT HIS CAREER as a NCO and as an officer, McNeil took special interest in those under his charge.[69] A young, would-be recruit named Don Duke received some good advice when he tried to join the Force in December 1949. Duke was advised by the Sergeant Major to go home and wait until the following January. "If you join now," said the Sergeant Major, "you'll be sent to Regina to shovel snow, look after the horses and do what are called fatigue duties." Young Duke took the advice, enjoyed Christmas and New Year's at home before joining the RCMP on January 6, 1950. It was S/M Stirling McNeil who gave him that sound advice. Duke had a very successful career, retiring with the rank of Superintendent.

Giving fatherly advice was a trait of McNeil's throughout his career. In 1964, David Holmes, a young recruit fresh out of training, reported to "L" Division where Supt. Stirling McNeil was the CO.

---

69 Editor's Note: the first female members were inducted into the RCMP in 1974, long after McNeil's retirement in 1966. This biography, therefore, refers mainly to the male members of McNeil's acquaintance on the Force.

*Supt. McNeil treated us recruits as if we were his own sons. If
he heard rumours of you running around with a number of girls
in town, he would call you in and have a fatherly chat about
it. On one occasion he called me in to advise me he had seen a
female picking me up at the front door and he felt she appeared
to be too young for me. I replied, 'But, sir, she is only 30 days
younger than me!'*

The girl became Holmes' wife two years later and McNeil was
there to give him another lesson on the morning of their wedding.
Holmes had done a little too much celebrating at a stag party arranged by his Sergeant. He was not expecting a visit from the CO.
Nevertheless, the Superintendent showed up to get rid of any liquor.

*I wasn't feeling too well that morning. Just imagine sitting over
a pail with beer, wine, rum and other liquors being poured into
it, to [then] be poured down the drain.*

And so the Superintendent provided a valuable lesson on the
consequences of over-drinking. Holmes retired as a Staff Sergeant
and resides in Charlottetown. The McNeils were always delighted
to attend the weddings of "L" Division "boys" and often kept in
touch, even after retirement.

A NUMBER OF McNeil's "boys" had distinguished careers in the
Force. A/Commr. Allan Burchill, who retired as OC "H" Division,
was one. McNeil was his model of what an RCMP officer should be.

S/Sgt. Carl MacLeod (Rtd.) still remembers the advice he received from Insp. McNeil.:

Insp. McNeil advised me to only speak when I was spoken to, work like I had never worked before and [that] I'd better like horses and manure because I was going to experience both in spades.

McNeil also wished him good luck, adding that he would need an abundance of it. The advice served MacLeod well; he is the subject of *A Master of Deception*, in which Robert Knuckle chronicles MacLeod's career as an undercover operator.

Insp. Gus Buziak (Rtd.) remembered well his first encounter with Insp. McNeil. It was a warm day at "Depot" Division as the recruits went about their duties. Buziak was tired and decided to grab a little rest by a tree. He fell into a deep sleep, suddenly awakened by someone kicking the soles of his shoes. Buziak looked up to see the gleaming boots of none other than Insp. McNeil. The inspector did not discipline Buziak, opting instead for a short lecture about not sleeping on the job.

A/Commr. Randy Schramm (Rtd.) remembered standing before Insp. McNeil at "Depot" Division. It was February 13, 1954 and McNeil was the officer in charge of training.

You had to get a medical certificate and the result of the criminal investigation check. Then I was paraded into Insp. McNeil's office. I didn't know how to march at that time but a Sergeant said, 'I'm going to march in. You just walk.'

Schramm, in civilian clothes, stood at attention while Insp. McNeil examined his application and supporting documents. McNeil seemed to take special interest in Schramm because he joined at age 24; most recruits were much younger—18 to 19 years old—and Schramm had given up a well-paying civilian job to join the RCMP for considerably less money, about $200 a month. Schramm went on to have an illustrious career. As McNeil had done before him, Schramm served in the North as well as on the prairies. An outstanding investigator throughout his career, he became Director of Criminal Investigations for the entire Force and retired with the rank of Assistant Commissioner.

McNEIL HAD ALWAYS been interested in community activities and sports, and was instrumental in forming baseball teams when he was at "Depot" Division. Schramm was one of the key pitchers and they had a number of good hitters, too. They had to be very polite and friendly with the teams they played against and there was no swearing. If their team was falling behind, McNeil would say, "Boys, it's about time you started hitting the ball." And sure enough, the RCMP team would start hitting and sometimes even came from behind to win.

McNeil believed that sports were a good recruiting tool. If the RCMP was good enough to beat the home team, some of those players might be interested in joining.

Randy Schramm was a troop-mate of Gar Clark, who joined the Force on February 2, 1954. Like Schramm, Clark was a pitcher.

Insp. McNeil attended all the team's games in communities not far from Regina like Marquis, Rouleau, Craik and Yellowgrass.

We had a hell of a good team. We played in some tournaments where there were 16 teams so you had a lot of THREE-*inning games to get down to the finals.*

Insp. McNeil would sit in the stands in civilian clothes and a baseball cap, cheering his team on. If anyone booed the RCMP team, McNeil soon had them rooting for the Mounties. Clark remembered one outing to Fortuna Air Base in North Dakota. The RCMP had played basketball against the Americans the previous winter and had tasted defeat. McNeil got to know the officer in charge of the base and bet him $2 the RCMP team could beat them in baseball. They won the game 2-1.

Robert Dempster also took his training in 1954.

Although our contacts with Insp. McNeil were limited, all of us were unanimous in our respect and admiration for the man. He was a gentleman and treated all with courtesy, regardless of rank.

Dempster recalled playing on the "Depot" baseball team for various sports days in towns around the province. "We had a very good team and as I recall, won every tournament save one of the dozen or so we entered."

While Gar Clark remembered the $2 bet won by the Inspector, Dempster says that on a trip to Crosby, North Dakota, McNeil told the customs officer they were going to play a baseball game against an Air Force team. McNeil bet the customs officer $2 that his "boys" would win the game. He collected on the way back home. "We were told that the US Air Force had flown in some 'ringers' to try and beat the Mounties."

Clark said Insp. McNeil was considerate. Because the team often returned home late at night, he directed that all team members were excused from 6:00 a.m. stable parade. "That was a big deal for us. It meant an extra hour's sleep and an unusual leisurely preparation for breakfast and the 9:00 parade."

SUPT. ERNIE MACAULAY (Rtd.) first met Insp. McNeil in about 1963 when MacAulay was a student at St. Dunstan's University, P.E.I. MacAulay was walking to his classroom behind a group of people that included the Rector and a number of other officials. McNeil saw him heading in the same direction and when they came to a doorway, McNeil waited and held the door open for him rather than keep up with the official party. MacAulay recalled how thoughtful Insp. McNeil had been to leave a conversation with senior university officials to hold open the door for an anonymous student.

MacAulay joined the RCMP on March 18, 1965. Although Supt. McNeil was the Commanding Officer and the only commissioned officer in "L" Division, he was away on duty when MacAulay was sworn in by a supreme court judge. However, McNeil told MacAulay he was not to leave the province without meeting him personally. MacAulay reported to the Superintendent in his office that evening. The Superintendent had obviously carefully read MacAulay's file and talked with him about members of his family as if he knew them personally.

McNeil told him it was his usual practice when swearing in recruits to take them to the window and say, "Take your last look at freedom, because as a member of the RCMP you will be required to have a pass to go anywhere." The Superintendent told MacAulay that his primary responsibility was the Force, that he would be abused and humiliated during training but that McNeil had also undergone the same treatment, and "Look at me now."

McNeil told MacAulay he did not want to see him back in P.E.I. until he had one year of service, but that when MacAulay was home on annual leave to come in for a chat. On many occasions during recruit training, MacAulay considered Supt. McNeil's advice and relied on it to get him through many difficult periods. At times he considered taking an easier route and purchasing his discharge, but persevered in his career as a Mountie. MacAulay retired as Superintendent in charge of the Richmond, B.C. detachment, and also served as Aide de Camp to four Lieutenants Governor of B.C. over a 21-year period.

In 1967, when MacAulay was stationed at Toronto International Airport Detachment, Supt. McNeil was travelling and had some time between flights. He came to the detachment, located in the basement of Terminal 1, and asked if there were any members from P.E.I. on duty. "When informed that I was on shift, he asked if I could come in and talk to him, which I gladly did." On another occasion, McNeil had enough time between flights to drive to

Belleville, ON and back for a visit with Cst. Wayne Harrocks, who had previously served in "L" Division.

S/SGT. JOHN ENTWISTLE (Rtd.) was 28 when he joined the RCMP in 1952, much older than most recruits.[70] It was unusual for a recruit to have much of a relationship with the Training Officer, but he had been a navigator in the Air Force for six years during the Second World War, so one day the Inspector called him into his office and began talking about flying. They had several such conversations. It was unusual in that the Inspector called him by his first name, John, but Entwistle said, "I called him 'sir.'"

Entwistle confessed he could have been in a lot of trouble when, returning from a night out in Regina, he smuggled a crock into the barracks—the ultimate sin.

> *Not feeling any pain, I was balancing along on a low steel railing next to the sidewalk when the Training Officer walked by. He must have seen the bottle even though it was wrapped. He laughed and said, 'Good evening, Entwistle—have a good time?' [Then] he kept right on going.*

The last time Entwistle saw McNeil was just before he left for "H" Division in Halifax, NS. McNeil called him into his office and said he was aware that Entwistle had relatives in Montreal and asked if he would like to spend a few days with them en route to

---

70   The maximum age for a recruit was 30.

Halifax. McNeil said he would tell "H" Division that Entwistle would be a few days late in arriving but did not tell them why.

Entwistle gave an illustration of the difference between McNeil and a certain unnamed CIB Officer. Interviewed as he arrived in Halifax, Entwistle said the CIB Officer greeted him with, "I don't expect you will be able to add to the reputation of the Force but make sure you don't do anything to detract from it."

Supt. Bill Schindeler (Rtd.) was a recruit at Rockcliffe when Insp. McNeil was the OIC of the Musical Ride.[71] Recruits were always told to salute an officer whenever they saw one. But Insp. McNeil had different instructions. He told the young recruits that because officers, including himself, walked past their work area several times a day, they would never get anything done if they stopped to salute every time. "Insp. McNeil told us just to keep our heads down and continue working." But that wasn't acceptable to another officer, who berated the recruits for not saluting. According to Schindeler, McNeil must have had a photographic memory. The two men had not seen each other for a decade, but McNeil still greeted him by name when they met again.

S/Sgt. Colin Craig (Rtd.) told stories that illustrated both Supt. McNeil's sense of humour, and his compassion and concern for his men.

---

71 Training for the Musical Ride had been moved to Rockcliffe that year because of an outbreak of hoof and mouth disease among livestock in Saskatchewan.

When Craig was promoted to Corporal:

The CO called me into his office to inform me of the promotion and to congratulate me. In the next breath he said 'If you don't cut the mustard, I can take it right back,' [and made] the motion of cutting his throat.

He added:

We have a son who is a severe hemophiliac. I was i/c Souris Detachment when Colin, Jr. was born and he often needed clotting infusions to stop the bleeding. Sometimes the roads to Charlottetown were blocked by snow in winter. The Superintendent was concerned that we [needed to] be in Charlottetown near the hospital. When the next rotation transfers came up, we went to Charlottetown. Supt. McNeil cared for his troops.

S/Sgt. Marshall MacKinnon (Rtd.) said Supt. McNeil was in a class by himself. "Although I don't know for sure, I would hazard a guess that he was not a highly educated man, but [he] was politically street-wise as far as the Force was concerned." McNeil knew the right answers and the short cuts necessary to do what needed doing.

During his term in P.E.I., McNeil had a real "problem child" in the lower NCO rank. McNeil wrote a letter to a neighbouring Commanding Officer, praising this member highly. McNeil added that since the NCO was in such a small division there was very little

Supt. A.S.McNeil, KSt.J, MiD
(photo credit: Frances Davies, ARPS).

opportunity for him, and a transfer might offer him more opportunity. McNeil asked MacKinnon to type out the letter, which he had written longhand.

After typing it, MacKinnon took the letter in to McNeil for his signature, whereupon the Superintendent asked, "What do you think of it, Staff"?

MacKinnon smiled but said nothing.

The Superintendent then told him, "Staff MacKinnon, when you have something to sell in this world, you do not run it down." The NCO was transferred.

EVEN IN RETIREMENT, McNeil continued to show interest in members of the Force. D/Commr. Don Wilson (Rtd.) met McNeil in Prince Edward Island. At one point, Wilson held the same position McNeil had once had—CO "L" Division. Whenever Wilson saw McNeil after he retired, the greetings were all along the same lines: "Donald! Continue to hear good things about you, m'boy."

S/Sgt. Dave Holmes (Rtd.) summed it up succinctly:

Supt. McNeil was the finest commanding officer I ever worked with in my 30 years in the RCMP. He treated us wet-behind-the-ears young recruits as one of his boys.

MCNEIL "RETIRES"

A portrait of Supt. McNeil, painted by P.E.I. artist Henry C. Purdy, presented to him as a retirement gift from the "L" Division NCOs.

AFTER NEARLY 35 years of service, Supt. McNeil and his wife Carolyn retired. Charlottetown did them proud. They attended an exhausting round of parties and presentations that did them much honour, and which was unprecedented for the RCMP on P.E.I. Articles in the newspapers praised his leadership, not only of the Force but of the organizations in which he was involved: Rotary Club, Royal Canadian Legion, RCAF Association, Masonic Lodge, P.E.I. Cancer Society, P.E.I. Safety Committee, Royal Canadian Air Cadets, Trinity Church, P.E.I. Polio Committee and Boy Scouts. He was also a director of the P.E.I. Mental Health Association and the Atlantic Provinces Corrections Association.

The editorial in the Charlottetown *Guardian* of May 25, 1966 was typical of the Island:

> *Superintendent A.S. McNeil, who retired yesterday as Officer Commanding 'L' Division, RCMP, had the misfortune of not being born in Prince Edward Island, but he has striven mightily to make up for this defect during his years of residence here, and there is no question about where he stands in the high regard of all our citizens.*

> *Since his transfer to Charlottetown in 1959, he has been an asset, not only to the Force, which he has so capably command-ed in this part of the Dominion, but to the whole community, associating himself as he has done with our service, church and welfare organizations, and giving leadership in many worth-while movements. We feel now that we have a right to claim him as one of our own, and Mr. McNeil himself—despite his wide experience in many other parts of the world—claims that this is by far the most delectable spot under the sun, the most congenial to his disposition, and the place where friendly con-tacts are ties that really bind and give enduring value to one's activities here below.*

> *We note that he plans some extensive travelling for his retire-ment; but like the homing pigeon, we're sure he won't forget his way back. We take this opportunity of telling him how much*

pleasure this thought gives to all his friends locally and through-
out the province.

To Superintendent R.P. Harrison who succeeds him as
Commanding Officer of 'L' Division, we extend our warmest
best wishes. Nor need we remind him that he is filling the shoes
of a mighty fine man.[72]

AFTER A WONDERFUL trip to Europe, Carolyn and Stirling moved
to Brentwood Bay, B.C. They missed the warmth of the people of
P.E.I., but not the winters.

Visitors to the first home the McNeils had ever owned were
greeted warmly. Carolyn was a gracious hostess and her husband
was always good for interesting conversation. Long-time family
friend Esther Farr, widow of the late A/Commr. Terry Farr, said
Carolyn McNeil was the "hostess with the mostest."

My goodness, Carolyn was elegant. She always had her hair
done up and she loved to wear a mink stole,[73] *and to attend*
functions at Government House. She was the epitome of a lady.

When Carolyn entertained, which was often, she always used
sterling silver and crystal.

Carolyn would always have brunches with the food laid out on
the table. She would decorate the table with two little penguins

---

72   *The Guardian*, May 25, 1966.

73   A gift from her son.

Carolyn and Stirling McNeil.

made of hard–boiled eggs, a little black hat, toothpicks for legs and olives for the feet. Carolyn set a beautiful table [and she] was very gracious. She was as elegant as Stirling was in manner and dress.

Terry Farr and Stirling were executives of the Corps of Commissionaires, St. John's Ambulance and Royal United Services Institute at different times. They were also on the Central Saanich Police Board, near Victoria. Terry often drove Stirling to meetings.

Esther Farr added that Stirling McNeil was a tall, handsome man with a good sense of humour. "When he met someone, he would shake hands and say, 'I don't care what others say about you, I think you're a fine fellow.'"

Party at Gov. House Victoria with Colonel Pip Holme. (photo credit: Brigadier General Steve McGowan). Note the Knight's Cross on McNeil's jacket.

ALTHOUGH RETIRED FROM the Force, McNeil maintained a keen interest in the goings-on of the active Force and its veterans, many of whom had also retired to Vancouver Island. McNeil was an active member and president of the RCMP Veterans Association, RCMP Retired Officers Association, a life member of the Canadian Association of Chiefs of Police, President of RCAF Officers, and President and Life Member of the Royal Vancouver Island United Services Institute (RUSI), an organization of retired military officers.

During his term as president, the Queen granted the USI the prefix "Royal," which had first been requested of Government House in Ottawa, but without success. Stirling, never the most patient of men, finally went to one of the members, a retired British Army Lieutenant General, who contacted Buckingham Palace.

Carolyn and Stirling, Knight of the Order of St. John investiture, 1990.

Stirling was the only Mountie to have served as president of all of these veteran's organizations. Victoria, B.C. media used him as a commentator on Royal visits and other occasions.

As an Officer of the Order of St. John, he continued his life-long interest and work for the Order. On February 7, 1990, in the thirty-ninth year of her reign, Her Majesty, the Sovereign Head of the Most Venerable Order of the Hospital of St. John of Jerusalem, made Stirling McNeil a Knight of the Order. At the time, he was the only living mounted policeman to be so honoured.

He also served on the local police commission, hospital board and as People's Warden at Brentwood College (Anglican) Chapel for many years. He had a simple, solid, unquestioning faith.

THERE IS CLEAR indication of the involvement of Stirling McNeil in key areas of development in the Force—"Air" Division, the Crime Lab and the Musical Ride. McNeil was involved in all three, and was pleased to attend a reunion for each one in 1988, though he was nearly 80 years old. He wrote about the reunions in a letter to *Scarlet & Gold:*

I was happy to attend three RCMP reunions this year. There was the Aviation Division reunion at Sidney, B.C. at the Patricia Bay Airport with approximately 175 attending, including four of the originals—P.B. Cox, D.W. Dawson, C.E. Gray and myself. This was to celebrate 50 years of the "Air" Division.

I flew to Regina and saw Commissioner Simmonds unveil a plaque marking 50 years of the operation of the RCMP crime laboratories. I was Post Adjutant there at the official opening of the Regina Lab. My recruit mate, the late Supt. Mason-Rooke, was OIC; the late Dr. Francis McGill, pathologist and my old pal, the late S/Sgt. Major Jim Robertson had been present at the opening. It was nice to reflect on old times and faces.

The Musical Ride reunion celebrated 100 years of the first Musical Ride performance in Regina. Former OICs in attendance were Joe Downey, Rod Williamson, Cliff Morin and the writer. It was interesting to recall that the Commissioner was a member of the Coronation Ride to London in 1953. Again the reunion committee did a marvelous job and a good time was had by all.

IN HIS RETIREMENT years, McNeil was a prolific writer, frequently sending letters to *Scarlet & Gold*. He often used those letters to recall men who had served with him. Referring to a previous article about a Royal Tour, McNeil said he had had a part in the 1939 and

1948 Royal Tours and was CO "L" Division when the Royals toured the Maritimes and the Province of Québec in 1964:

> *It took nearly a year of prior planning by the Royal Tour Committee and then we had them for the better part of five days. All police, armed forces personnel and the public were most co-operative, so this segment of the tour went off splendidly.*

A detailed account of the Royal Tour had been written by Don Fraser, who had served under McNeil in Prince Edward Island. McNeil wrote about Fraser.

> *On assuming command of "L" Division in July 1959, I was pleased to see Fraser stationed there. Because of his good work with us, I was able to promote him to Division Sergeant Major and was indeed sorry to lose him later to pension.*

McNeil's reference to Fraser was typical of his interest in members who had served with him. In 1980, for example, McNeil enlisted the help of *Scarlet & Gold* to plan the 50th reunion of his own recruit contemporaries. He asked the veterans' publication for help locating still-living members of the group.

> *We appreciate because of age and distance, a reunion would be impossible at this time. However, with the close co-operation of ex–S/M James Robinson of Regina we are trying to contact all members of this group and get passport photos of all surviving members and try for a composite photo. It will at least indicate*

our present appearance in spite of the lapse of time since our recruit days. We have already had indications that some 20 are dead, including the late 10946 Harrison and George Campbell who was murdered on duty in Banff in 1935.

McNeil often wrote to *Scarlet & Gold* about his former colleagues. In 1983, he commented on an article that mentioned people he knew, among them Joe Olsen, when he was a member of the *St. Roch* crew, and the late Sgt. Joe Leatham, whom McNeil knew well from his days in "F" Division.[74] He also identified ex-D/S/Sgt. S. H. Hermanson, who was the detective in Moose Jaw in McNeil's brief stay in that Saskatchewan city. He remembered Major Tom Quirk, whom he had met in the early days of the war when Quirk was with the Army and he was with the RCAF. McNeil said he and Quirk had been friends for years, noting Quirk had served as a constable in the RCMP in Peace River Sub-Division when McNeil was OC.

MORE THAN THIRTY years after he retired, McNeil could still vividly recall the early days of his career. One story concerned the exploits of Constable Louis Schodat, who got himself in trouble while escorting a prisoner on a train. Something of a ladies' man, Schodat noticed two attractive girls sitting together, and an elderly, bearded gentleman seated opposite them. Hoping to strike up a conversation with the girls, Schodat coveted the gentleman's seat and asked him to move. The man refused. Schodat promptly snatched him up by the goatee and hauled him off to a different seat! Little did

74   Leatham was the much-respected farrier at "Depot" in the fall of 1931.

"McNeil of the Mounties," *Ottawa Citizen*, July 21, 2001.

he know that the gentleman happened to be a senator from the Gravelbourg area of Saskatchewan. The senator used his influence to have the porter stop the train at the next station, where a phone call was placed to RCMP headquarters. Schodat was in hot water, and, after an investigation, he left the Force.

MCNEIL TOLD ANOTHER story about some of the early officers of the Force, one he'd been told by Huey Matheson, who had joined as a trumpeter. Matheson was the son of a well-thought-of Staff Sergeant and had been commissioned as a Sub-Inspector in Regina.

As part of his indoctrination training, Matheson had attended what is believed to be the first Western Canada conference of commanding officers. Several well-known characters were also there, including A/Commr. Bertie King. Apparently, King said off-handedly, "What the Force needs is some old-time Sergeant Majors with army service background—good disciplinarians, smart-looking and not too many bloody brains." An awkward pause followed this remark. Into the silence, Matheson said sweetly, "The reason there's none of that breed left is that they're all now Assistant Commissioners." According to Matheson, you could've heard a pin drop.

McNEIL ALSO RECALLED the story of a member who became OC at Winnipeg. He was a great one to "dry snap"[75] his pistol, and was, in fact, a world champion revolver shot. A member from the orderly room who came into the CO's office to get some papers signed was startled to look up right into the muzzle of a gun. He threw up his hands in shock, papers falling like leaves in a tornado.

"Get out of the road you fool!" barked the CO, "I've got my eye on a fly!"

The startled member went right to D.K. Martin, the divisional Sergeant Major at the time, and said, "The CO is crazy!" Then he thought better of it and amended the accusation—"Crazy about shooting, sir."

---

75   To "dry fire" a gun with no ammunition as practice.

McNeil also told an anecdote about A/Commr. Tom Dan, known for his feats of strength and boxing ability, a story related to him by Insp. Martin, who had been the divisional Sergeant Major in Winnipeg.

If a citizen had a complaint about the Force, the policy was to have the Sergeant Major escort the citizen into the Assistant Commissioner's office. The Sergeant Major would salute smartly and say, 'Sir, I have so-and-so to speak to you. He has a complaint about the Force.' The citizen would be left standing in front of the seated officer for several minutes, probably wondering what to do next.

Suddenly, A/Commr. Dan would shoot his hand out as a gesture of welcome. The fellow would take Dan's hand and, before you could say Jack Robinson, he had the complainant halfway across the desk, knocking an inkwell over in the process. A/Commr. Dan would mumble something about how clumsy he was and pretend to mop up the ink. By this time the poor chap would be so humiliated he would almost forget about his complaint, excuse himself and get out of the office.

Martin observed this procedure several times and said to himself, 'You'd never catch me like that.'

A short time later, Martin received his commission. The buzzer rang for him to come into the CO's office.

'So, I came in, saluted him smartly and took one pace forward. The CO paused and went through the same old routine, signing some papers. All of a sudden his hand shot out and he said, 'Congratulations on your commission, Martin.'

I was so dumbfounded, my hand went out to grasp his and before I knew it I was in his lap on the desk with the inkwell whirling around. I was so shaken I could hardly get over it. And I thought afterwards, 'My God, even after seeing that done so many times, I fell into the trap myself.'

WHEN MCNEIL JOINED in 1931, the Commissioner was James Howden MacBrien, who had been a soldier and a policeman. He had served in the militia, the North West Mounted Police and the South African Constabulary from 1901 to 1906. At the outbreak of the First World War, he was a Staff Officer in the Canadian Army and rose to become Chief of the General Staff, Overseas Forces, 1919 to 1920. MacBrien presided over the formation of Canada's National Defence Department in 1927 and was appointed Commissioner of the RCMP in 1931, the year Stirling McNeil joined the Force.

There is little doubt Commr. MacBrien had an impact on McNeil's career. MacBrien was the first Commissioner to recognize the value of aircraft in police work and was instrumental in forming the RCMP "Air" Division, in which McNeil served.

As a Duty Driver in Regina, McNeil occasionally drove Commissioner Aylesworth Bowen Perry. The next Commissioner during

McNeil's service was Stuart Taylor Wood, whose father, Zachary Taylor Wood, served in the North West Mounted Police from 1885 to 1915. The younger Wood had been a military man, serving as a Lieutenant in the cavalry in France and Belgium during the First World War. Upon returning to Canada after the war, he served in Yukon as justice of the peace, coroner, sheriff, games inspector and customs officer.

During his time as Commissioner of the RCMP, from 1938 to 1951, Wood initiated many changes. Through 1945 and 1946, he established a system of registration for aliens and dealt with espionage cases (i.e. Igor Gouzenko).[76] In the North, he initiated new policing detachments. He organized an RCMP Band, which existed until 1994.

Commr. Wood established the first RCMP scientific laboratory (the crime lab) and a museum in Regina. He also established a horse breeding station at Fort Walsh, Saskatchewan. He improved wireless communications and broadcasting, and instituted a preventive training program for youth. Just as Commr. MacBrien's interest in aircraft likely influenced Stirling McNeil, it can be speculated that Commr. Wood's innovations and his pioneering work in community policing also had an influence.

Commr. Wood retired to Fort Walsh, where the McNeil family saw another side to this stern disciplinarian. On a summer holiday visit to the historic fort, the McNeils were warmly welcomed by

---

76 "On Sept. 5, 1945, just after the end of the Second World War, a Russian cipher clerk named Igor Gouzenko fled the Soviet Embassy in Ottawa with 109 documents proving the existence of a Soviet spy ring in Canada. His revelations reverberated throughout the world and helped to ignite the Cold War." "The Gouzenko Affair," CBC Digital Archives, http://www.cbc.ca/archives/topic/the-gouzenko-affair. Accessed May 4, 2016.

the former Commissioner, who invited them to lunch and offered Cam his daughter's horse to ride. Cam had a great gallop until the horse saw a rattlesnake and almost threw him over his head onto the coiled snake!

McNEIL WAS GIVEN his Commission in 1951 by Commr. L.H. Nicholson, whom he had known during the Second World War. Nicholson had been a Lieutenant-Colonel in the Provost Corps, while McNeil had been a Wing Commander in the Air Force. They were the most senior officers from their respective services to return to the RCMP after the war.

There is no doubt of the affinity between McNeil and Commissioner Nicholson. Nicholson was a man of principle, who resigned in 1959 due to a disagreement with the federal government over sending 50 mounted police troops to control a labour dispute in Newfoundland. The RCMP is not an autonomous organization so federal approval was necessary for the additional resources. It was refused on the grounds that it would disrupt policing elsewhere. Nicholson did not agree. He regarded the government's decision as a breach of faith that prevented the Force from fulfilling its con- tractual obligations to Newfoundland.

McNeil also served under Commissioners C.E. Rivett-Carnac, C. W. Harvison and George B. McClellan. McNeil apparently had good relations with all Commissioners and, even in retirement, made courtesy calls on the serving Commissioners.

According to Supt. Cliff MacDonald (Rtd.), officers were a close-knit group and few in number. In the 1960s, there were prob- ably less than 100 or so commissioned officers in the Force and they all knew each other. McNeil had a particularly close relationship with his last Commissioner, George McClellan.

One of McNeil's favourite expressions was, "Get on with it." And when he wanted things done, he wanted them done, right away. One of his top NCOs in "L" Division, S/Sgt. Marshall MacKinnon, said that if Supt. McNeil wanted something, he would simply pick up the phone and call Commr. McClellan. He would get verbal approval and would then write to the OIC of a particular branch or directorate to make his request, adding that it had already been approved by the Commissioner. McNeil usually got what he wanted for his Division.

Just as he had done during active service in the RCMP, McNeil treasured his friends in retirement, old and new, and "got on with it."

LIEUTENANT-COLONEL CECIL BEREZOWSKI (Rtd.) met Supt. McNeil in 1985. By the time they met, McNeil was an older man and had trouble driving at night, so Berezowski drove him to evening RUSI meetings. Berezowski recalled many pleasant chats with McNeil. In 1989, Berezowski was named Chairman of the National Defence Committee of the Federation of Military and United Services Institutes of Canada (FMUSIC). In that capacity, he wrote many briefs on defence strategy and testified before the Commons Committee on Peacekeeping Operations. It was highly technical information, but McNeil took a keen interest.

Colonel Berezowski said of McNeil:

He was a very striking individual. Of course, he was physically very tall and very erect, like a flagpole almost. In a group he stood out head and shoulders above everybody else because he was so tall. He was quite physically fit and lean and muscular. There was no fat on him; he was a striking figure of a man. In some respects, he was a giant among ordinary people, very striking. The veterans respected him because he knew his stuff, he had proven himself, and when he did speak he was gracious and spoke with wisdom.

C/Supt. Vince Cain (Rtd.) was a young Constable on an inspection team that visited "L" Division in P.E.I. in 1963. He had heard all about Supt. McNeil and his reputation for being involved in the community and meeting people on the street.

Supt. McNeil was a huge man—big in body and personality. You couldn't help but like the man because of that. The other thing that struck me was his eyes. When he talked to you, he came very close to you and he hung on every word you said. He wasn't talking about himself at all. He just thought about you as a person and he would extract everything out of you.

McNeil had a unique personality and Cain often thought that he would be great at getting statements from criminals and witnesses "because he impressed you so much."

Many years passed before Cain was to see McNeil again when both were retired in Victoria and members of the RCMP Veterans

Association. McNeil would come through the door and everybody knew him and he knew them; he would go through the whole room shaking hands with everybody.[77]

C/Supt. Harry Nixon (Rtd.) always found McNeil to be very much a gentleman.

> *He was a big man. He was ramrod straight—handsome. He had a great head of hair. He was very couth. He was very rigid in his appearance and in the way he did his paperwork. And he was just meticulous in his presentation and his uniform.... very much of the old school. You had to do things properly.... You couldn't get anybody any better. He stood out. He was big and impressive and he stood out in a room. His manner of speaking was forceful.*

Murray Ross (Rtd.) joined the Force in 1956 and served in "K" Division, the Province of Alberta. He was sent to Peace River where a new barracks had just been built. McNeil, then an Inspector, was the OC and seemed to take special interest in Ross because he had skills as an aircraft maintenance man and had a pilot's licence. At one time Ross had worked for famed aviator Max Ward. Ross went on to "Air" Division at the urging of McNeil. McNeil told him, "Don't refuse. If you do, the OIC will never ask you again." Ross took the advice. While working for McNeil, Ross said he

---

77   He used to call Cain "Mr. Coroner." Cain retired from the RCMP and joined the B.C. Coroner's Service, eventually becoming chief coroner.

spent considerable time "shaking hands with doorknobs" on patrol. However, he also followed his OC's advice and worked closely with kids in the community. He attended hockey games in uniform to cheer the kids on. After that, kids would meet him on the street and say, "Hi, Constable." Rapport with the kids in the community of Viking, Alberta, was very helpful. A number of kids were breaking windows. Ross gathered them together and took them to a gravel pit and invited the kids to start digging to make a swimming hole. Soon parents and siblings were involved too. "It was a way of keeping kids out of trouble" and was just the kind of project that McNeil would have supported wholeheartedly.

LIEUTENANT-COMMANDER STIRLING ROSS (Rtd.) remembered Stirling McNeil when both were members of RUSI. In fact, it was McNeil who asked him to join RUSI, noting that Ross was qualified because of his naval service. The year was 1975 and Stirling McNeil was president of the Victoria RUSI chapter.

Ross recalled having met Stirling McNeil many years earlier when Ross was a boy of about nine in 1939. McNeil had come to take a course at Rockcliffe, Ontario, the RCMP establishment near Ottawa (also known as "N" Division). Ross's father had come from White Lake, near Renfrew, about 60 miles northwest of Ottawa. Together, they went to a cemetery to visit various graves of Stirling's family, who had been buried at White Lake. On the visit to the cemetery, Ross sat next to McNeil in the car, likely a Model T Ford with running boards. McNeil was an imposing man. "I felt like a dwarf sitting beside him."

The next time he remembered seeing McNeil was in 1966 when he and his wife went on a camping trip to Prince Edward Island. They stopped in to see Stirling and Carolyn, who were very hospitable, "as they always were." Ross's final Navy posting was to Esquimalt, B.C., in 1973. He retired there as a Lieutenant Commander two years later, and that's when he again made contact with the McNeils, whom he and his wife often visited.

To say that the McNeils made friends wherever they were posted is an understatement. When he took the RCMP Musical Ride to California in 1952, he made friends among many celebrities, and he and Charlton Heston exchanged Christmas cards for years. The McNeils received as many as 400 Christmas cards every year.

ALTHOUGH A/COMMR. CORT MacDonnell (Rtd.) never served with Stirling McNeil, his father did. "My dad had great respect for him, as did many members of the Force. He was the ultimate gentleman."

McNeil's brief playing career with the Saskatchewan Roughriders in 1931 and again in 1937 was honoured at a ceremony in Regina in 1989 or 1990 when he and other veterans were driven onto the field at half-time. MacDonnell had the pleasure of meeting McNeil at that event. Like McNeil, MacDonnell was a member of the RCMP Veterans Association, and they often had conversations about a broad spectrum of things past and present. McNeil continued to be interested in the progress and changes the Force was facing and thought of the RCMP as if it were family, "…members of his era are intensely proud of the organization and what it did."

THE LANGLEY YEARS

His ADVANCED AGE and failing health prompted Stirling McNeil and his wife Carolyn to leave their pleasant home at Brentwood Bay on Vancouver Island to move to the acreage home of their daughter Barbara and her husband Stephen Price in Langley, a Vancouver suburb. The house had been renovated to provide them with a suite.

Stephen Price joined the RCMP in 1971 and married Barbara McNeil in 1973. He was the son of an RCMP Superintendent, but his father and Barbara's were very different; the Price family was very private: the McNeil family was very outgoing. Stephen left the Force in 1978, attended university and became a lawyer, operating a practice in Langley, B.C. "The running joke when we set up the suite was that there was no question my mother-in-law was welcome. The question was, 'Did she have to bring him?'" Stephen quickly added, "Yes, we got along pretty well." But Stephen's affection for his mother-in-law was obvious. "She was the finest person—and she was my mother too."

The suite was designed to be totally self-sufficient and the Prices saw the McNeils at least every few days. Stirling and Carolyn were very proud of their four grandchildren, Barbara's two children in B.C. and Cam's two in Ontario.

Stephen said his father-in-law was in the Force at the right time.

You could have set Stirling into any number of similar activities anytime from the 17th Century on. Nothing after his era. He could have fit in on the March West; he could have been exploring Africa, whatever. But he was a creature of his time. He didn't have a great life [before the RCMP] but he was very self-reliant and self-contained. How do you go and live in the Arctic and fish and chase dogs—or do dogsled patrols? I don't know. It's nothing I could ever have done.

Stirling's son Cam agreed, but added that Stirling's leadership qualities and concern for people and the rule of law are timeless and relevant, now more than ever.

STIRLING AND CAROLYN McNeil adjusted to their new life in Langley, but they missed their friends from Vancouver Island and living in a community where neighbours were close by. Stirling kept up his affiliation with the RCMP Veterans Association and often visited the Langley Detachment, where he was welcomed with open arms. The OIC, Supt. Cliff MacDonald—a native of Prince Edward Island—and his staff were always glad to see him. McNeil was a very popular visitor. Bonnie Schneider and Lainie Goddard in particular took a real fancy to him because he was so interesting.

*Bonnie would go out and get some date squares or cookies or
doughnuts from Tim Horton's if she knew McNeil was coming.
It was like they were setting up for a celebration. They would sit
in the boardroom and listen to McNeil's stories.*

McNeil always told stories in a way the staff knew that they
were true, stories about his time in the North, his time with the
Musical Ride and his command in P.E.I. And they hung on every
word. He talked about his time with the RCAF during the Second
World War, but MacDonald added:

*If somebody asked him, 'Did you fly a plane?' it would have been
very simple for him to say, 'Well, yes, I did.' Instead he would
reply, 'Look, I wasn't smart enough to fly a plane', or something
like that. The truth of the matter is that McNeil was a good
pilot but only visual* [78] *versus flying in cloud.* [79] *He was so honest.*

Supt. MacDonald[80] said if McNeil were an officer in the Force
today he would be a very progressive thinker:

*I've known a lot of officers through the years who were most
hard-nosed about things and more focused on discipline. Stirling*

---

78 Visual Flying Rules (VFR).

79 Instrument Flying Rules (IFR).

80 Supt. MacDonald (Rtd.) worked on a pilot project for the Force, co-coordinating
Community Safety Officers (CSOs). D/Comm. Gary Bass, C.O. of "E" Division sup-
ports the idea of having officers available for community work, acknowledging
that serious incidents such as homicides drain communities of police personnel.
CSOs are drawn from auxiliary police officers and volunteers. They wear a uniform similar to the RCMP but with a different shoulder patch. They do not carry
guns. So far, there are fewer than 20 CSOs, stationed in several B.C. communities.

was a very disciplined man, but he understood the weaknesses that other people have—and, y'know, you couldn't help but respect him for that. He was the type of guy who came across as very helpful and aware of community issues and problems. He would have been a very modern thinker if he was working in this era. He was a straight shooter.

Bonnie Schneider had warm recollections of Supt. McNeil:

The first time I met him, I thought 'Oh, my goodness, he's so easy to talk to.' He was jovial and a real gentleman. He would call us 'ladies of the office'. He was quite a jokester and he made you feel like you had known him for 20 years. He was part of the family.

McNeil wanted to be around RCMP members; he wanted to know what was going on and liked to voice his opinions about police matters to Supt. MacDonald. McNeil visited once or twice a month, and Bonnie and Supt. MacDonald sometimes went to the McNeils' home in Langley. There they saw beautiful artifacts, gifts that had been given to McNeil from places he had served and "so much RCMP memorabilia it was just like a museum."

Lainie Goddard added that McNeil was very proud of the RCMP. "He was proud of family, including his four grandchildren, but … when he talked about the Mounties, it was with great pride."

AT THIS TIME, the McNeils could no longer function without assistance. They were fortunate to obtain the services of a professional caregiver, a kindly woman named Anne Schroeder, whom McNeil regaled with his stories of the Force. Anne recalled how special it was for McNeil to attend Remembrance Day services. She would get him ready for the occasion by trimming his moustache—she was the only one allowed to trim it! Anne would then polish his shoes and his buttons, and make sure his blue blazer looked good. She would take a day off from her regular job as a caregiver to take him to Remembrance Day services.

As well as assisting Mrs. McNeil in the kitchen and sometimes serving Mr. McNeil breakfast in his room, Anne often wrote letters for him, sometimes to the Commissioner of the RCMP or to a man in South Africa who had served with McNeil in the RCMP.

The McNeils were very generous and supported a number of charities. Under Mr. McNeil's direction, Anne mailed his old football team sweater to the Saskatchewan Sports Hall of Fame *(see p. 32)*.

Carolyn McNeil's death in 2001 took a toll on Stirling McNeil. Anne recalled that "He missed Carolyn every single day. He had adored her. The McNeils had what marriages should be. They were very happily married." Barbara added:

She was his best friend. She really was the one who swabbed him up. She would write his speeches for him; she would patiently listen and have him practice all his talks. She was a very gracious hostess. He was a diamond in the rough in the beginning, but between the two of them they were a very good team. They loved people and they loved Canada. They were honourable, religious, caring people, and fabulous parents.

A RETURN TO "DEPOT"

McNEIL'S HEALTH DETERIORATED quickly after that. He had great difficulty with circulation to his feet, possibly stemming from frostbite he suffered during his service in the North. But McNeil never complained. Ultimately both legs were amputated. Though that would have been devastating to anyone, Stephen said his father-in-law bore it well. "He adapted. He never, ever felt sorry for himself." McNeil's attitude was that life was what it was and "you've got to carry on." Said Stephen, "He always did."

The staff at Langley detachment threw a surprise party for their OIC Supt. MacDonald, to celebrate his 35 years in the RCMP. They brought Stirling McNeil in his wheelchair. She said, "Stirling was proud as punch in his blue blazer."

Supt. MacDonald recalled one outing that had special significance for McNeil. The RCMP had taken over part of the former military base at Chilliwack, B.C. for use as a training centre. MacDonald had made arrangements to pick up McNeil and take him to the facility.

We went down to the training facility, parked outside and I took him in.... He was just absolutely flabbergasted.... He was so happy to see this place and to see the RCMP in training. He was totally absorbed with it.

It was to be one of the last outings for McNeil, who missed Carolyn terribly. "I can hardly wait to be with her," MacDonald recalled him saying. "He was a very loyal kind of person. His wife meant everything to him."

McNeil was stoic about pain. His daughter Barbara was the one who would notice when he was uncomfortable and call for help at the care centre where he spent nine months. It was very painful for him when he had to be transferred using an amputee's sling.

At the end of the amputation the nerves were active, so if the sling touched him with his weight on it, it would be excruciatingly painful. I was there once and I noticed him wince. I said, 'Oh, please put him down.' They put him down and had him repositioned because he was biting down and hanging on and it must have been hugely painful and he wouldn't let them know. There wouldn't be a squeak from him that he was in pain. He never complained. He said to us years ago after he had to put his aunt in extended care that 'If I go into extended care, that's fine—don't you worry about it.'

All the staff really liked him. His mother and sisters had been nurses and he valued nursing. One of the nurses said he never failed to say thank you for anything they did for him. He was always very appreciative of them, was glad to see them and was always upbeat.

Barbara recalled her father's last day.

Dad got pneumonia and when I went in he would be breathing funny. In the last few days he was checked by different doctors. They called pneumonia 'old man's friend' and in the end, he slipped away with it.

I sat with him. I called my husband and he came over. We sat with him from noon until after midnight when he passed away. It was very quiet. I would hold his hand or have my hand on his chest. Sometimes we would read to him and his breathing just got slower and finally it stopped....it was very gentle. All the staff came in to see him—to say goodbye.

It was June 23, 2004. Stirling McNeil was 95.

DURING THEIR TIME in Langley, Stirling McNeil and his wife Carolyn attended St. George's Anglican Church in the heart of historic Fort Langley. The priest was Reverend Pam Worthington, an outstanding, articulate and compassionate woman who developed a great fondness for the McNeils. On first meeting them, Rev.

Worthington noted that "Stirling presented himself very genuinely but incredibly, outstanding in the sense that [he] was a presence, a physical presence."

Her predominant memory was of Stirling being wheeled into church in a wheelchair, always sitting up very proudly. "There was no slouch with Stirling McNeil, that's for sure." His presence was magnetic. He had charisma. He always wore a tie to church and often some of the medals that he had earned. "It was never in an ostentatious way but in a quiet way, as if to say, 'This is part of who I am.'"

The priest had warm words for the McNeil family. "My main memory is of him sitting in his wheelchair with his family next to him. They were always sitting together—a very loving, gentle family. Just the epitome of gentleness."

Rev. Worthington sometimes visited homes of parishioners, and chuckled, "Whether they wanted me to or not." The McNeils would always invite her to stay for tea, which, she said, was "just short of Empress Hotel service with tea, little biscuits or carrot cake, with doilies and beautiful little cups and saucers. It was a liturgy."

McNeil made an impact on people he met in church. She told the story of a boy named Ethan, age 11. Every Sunday that McNeil came to church, Ethan would run to him to give him a big hug as though he were the most important person in the world.

As with most people he met, McNeil soon found common ground upon which to base a conversation. He almost always spoke in terms of the other person's interest. Such was the case with Rev. Pam Worthington. She had an interesting career. An American, she had served as a probation officer and sheriff's deputy in El

Dorado County, California. She was a crack shot and knew a great deal about firearms. She and McNeil talked about that and shared personal experiences.

Rev. Worthington knew firsthand of McNeil's suffering and described it eloquently.

I have been a priest for 22 years and I have never seen such a sad unfolding of tragedy. I don't believe Stirling had diabetes but whatever he had caused very poor circulation. He had sores on his legs that would not heal and it was because of them that he was in a wheelchair. He was not able to walk because of it. And finally it became apparent to doctors that the only recourse left was amputation. So they amputated. I cannot recall the number of amputations he had, but over the course of a year, this proud, proud man went from being 6'4" to being in a hospital with increasing amputations, which removed his lower torso all the way eventually up to his trunk. So he was immobile on his bed, on his back. His eyesight had gone and he could scarcely see. His hearing was so poor that you had to shout, but his mind was sharp and clear. He was in a prison—a prison of decreasing size. It just broke our hearts.

Rev. Worthington said Stirling McNeil lived in a time and a manner that the only thing that limited him was his integrity, and it he used wisely.

I have an abiding precious memory of his spirit, unquenchable in the face of humiliation. He was reduced to total helplessness

at the end but he bore that without complaint and the dignity
with which he lived his life. I was honoured to know him and
the people of St. George's Parish felt the same way.

At his funeral service, Rev. Worthington said:

As we journey through life, we encounter, if we're lucky, that rare
person whose life touches us with pure gold. We're enriched by that
encounter—we're blessed, and we're better than we were before.

At the burial service, held later in Regina, the eulogy was deliv-
ered in the historic RCMP Chapel by his granddaughter Melissa
Kane, MLIS and his grandson, Stirling McNeil, BA. As the 2000
Firefighter Challenge World Champion, 6′6″"Little Stirling" is a
worthy successor to his grandfather. Alexander Stirling McNeil—
Roughrider, pilot, and Mountie, was buried next to Carolyn, his wife
of 63 years, at the historic RCMP cemetery at "Depot" Division,
Regina, Saskatchewan. Cam was very touched by the service.

Dad had been a Sergeant Major; the Sergeant Major was there.
Dad had been Adjutant; the Adjutant was there. Dad had been
Training Officer, the Training Officer was there—all of them in
red serge. A very thoughtful tribute …. The turnout of veterans
was wonderful. Two horses and riders in North West Mounted
Police uniforms stood guard outside the chapel.

The Roughriders played in Regina that day and won. Stirling
would have been pleased.

The markers for Stirling and Carolyn McNeil at the RCMP cemetery.
Photograph courtesy of Sawatzky Studios.

Barbara says it was fitting that her parents were buried in Regina at the RCMP cemetery. "We knew for years that was where they wanted to be. It was a beautiful, tranquil place, very quiet."[81]

Stirling McNeil will be remembered for many things. He did not care about politics; he cared about the Force, and mostly about people. People from far and wide mourned McNeil and many told his family that he would never be forgotten because of the things he had done and the way he lived his life. Prime Minister Paul Martin and RCMP Commissioner Zaccardelli both wrote personal and touching letters of condolence.

Supt. Alexander Stirling McNeil (Rtd.), KStJ., MiD, lived long and well enough to become a true Canadian legend.

---

81 Stirling McNeil's obituary—"Colourful Mountie will rest here," written by Barb Pacholik—was front page news in the Regina *Leader-Post* and was picked up by the Canadian Press and reprinted in the *Ottawa Citizen*.

EPILOGUE 1

McNeil Family Memories

BARBARA PRICE (NÉE McNeil) went to elementary school in four provinces. Her brother Cam spent only one year in Peace River, Alberta, then went to Concordia College in Edmonton for grades 11 and 12. The high school in Peace River was very old and not in good condition. At times there were snowdrifts in the Grade 9 classroom; students sometimes wore mukluks to school. Barbara attended grades 5 to 8 in Peace River, and Grades 9 and 10 in Prince Edward Island, then a boarding school, Kings Edgehill, in Windsor, Nova Scotia. That school was chosen because the family felt that if they were posted back West again it was important for her to have a West-approved junior matriculation. Nova Scotia had both junior and senior matriculation but Prince Edward Island did not.

When Barbara's father retired to Vancouver Island, she joined her parents in British Columbia, where she worked for the B.C. Ferry Corporation at its head office in Victoria for a year. She then she went back East to graduate, obtaining a Bachelor of Science degree from Mount Allison University in Sackville, New Brunswick. Barbara spent much of her professional life as a Registered Dietitian, and became Director of Dietetics at the Glendale-Tillicum facility, a 474-bed hospital in Saanich, near Victoria. It was quite a coup for her to be the person in charge there. The technology was so new they didn't have recipes developed yet, and she helped develop them.

Barbara met her future husband, Stephen Price, when she and her family were invited to a wedding. Stephen told his mother, "I think I've met the woman I'm going to marry."

However, they had to wait a little. Stephen, following in the footsteps of his father, had joined the RCMP and they had to wait two years to be married. And so Stirling McNeil walked down the aisle with his daughter on his left, which is the opposite of what happens in civilian weddings. Military tradition dictates that an officer must have his sword hand free at all times to ward off any foe. (There were none!)

Stirling and Carolyn could be counted on to support the young family, especially after their grandchildren came along:

> *If we got a chance to get away when the boys were little, mom and dad would drive up and babysit for us. They would literally expect a list from us that they were to accomplish. He would say, 'Give me a to-do list. [And] if the to-do list wasn't long enough, granddad would find other things to do.'*

Barbara described her parents as loving, gentle, caring grandparents. She recalled some wonderful times, including a lovely trip with them to Salt Spring Island (in the Gulf Islands of British Columbia) and to Tofino, on the west coast of Vancouver Island.

CAMPBELL MCNEIL'S FATHER was his hero.

I had scarlet fever as a kid, my ribs were broken and re-set. I had a heart murmur. My dad never said anything, but I had a feeling he wanted me to be an athlete like him. I always had the feeling I could never live up to my dad in several areas.

Though he may not have been an athlete like his father, Cam also flew planes and had a very successful career. He became an engineer and designed a ground source heat pump that won national acclaim when the National Research Council found it to be the most efficient in the world.

Stirling McNeil struggled academically and had to get his senior matriculation by correspondence. While stationed in the North, he studied on dog patrols and in his spare time, and held the view that a university degree was both an incredible achievement and a valuable one. In his younger years, McNeil had sacrificed his own education for the need to work to support his siblings.

Cam found academics came easily to him. He attended Concordia College in Edmonton[82] and went on to the engineering program at Dalhousie University. The fact that he had graduated from university seemed more important to Cam's father than his later development of the heat pump, or his contributions to world-class environmental emergency computer systems, or his management of the $360 million Federal/Provincial Conservation and

---

82   Now Concordia University, of which Cam has been the longest serving regent on the board.

Renewable Energy Demonstration Agreements, which resulted in programs such as R2000 super energy efficient homes.

Still active in retirement, Cam has flown as a missionary pilot to Indigenous villages in northern Ontario, and helped initiate World Heritage status for the Rideau Canal. He chaired the organization of the 2009 National Rivers Conference and was awarded the National River Conservation Award of Merit.

The athlete in Cam's family is his son Stirling, who played football for Bishop's University and, in 2000, became World Champion in the Firefighter Challenge. Cam and Uldine, his wife of 43 years, were also blessed with a daughter, Melissa, now a senior librarian at Geologic Survey of Canada, and six grandchildren. When his mother, Carolyn, first met Uldine, she told Cam that Uldine was a "keeper." Carolyn was seldom wrong in her judgments of people.

Family was very important to Stirling and Carolyn and they passed it on to subsequent generations by example. They travelled from Brentwood Bay on Vancouver Island to Ottawa or Vancouver for all the major events of their grandchildren's lives: births, baptisms, confirmations, university graduations and marriages.

Cam and Uldine and their children kept in close touch with the senior McNeils. At least once a year and often more, they flew their airplanes from Ottawa to B.C. The three generations delighted in travelling together, too—to England and Scotland (including the ancestral home on the desolate Isle of Barra, Outer Hebrides), to Hawaii twice, on a cruise from Alaska, to San Francisco and New Orleans. They also went around the world with Uldine and Cam, cruising from Singapore to Bombay.

Before they went to Scotland, Cam and his dad met the

chieftain of Clan McNeil: Ian, an American professor of law at Princeton. Ian and Stirling got on very well, and agreed that, given the family ancestry of pirates and sheep-stealers, it was they who were the "black sheep" and on the wrong side of the law. Ian gave Stirling a note to the keeper of the McNeil ancestral home in Kisimul Castle in Castlebay, Barra.

Badge of Clan McNeil of Barra.

The trip from the mainland was unforgettable. A piper played on the wing of the bridge as the vessel left Oban with the echo resounding from the rock cliffs. On the long trip out, Stirling and Cam talked to an officer in a kilt. He asked why they were going to Barra. "There is nothing on Barra, ye know." Stirling replied that he was returning with his family, the first in five generations to return. Just before they started down the gangway, the officer ran up, kilt flying, and ordered the piper ashore, where the family was piped ashore to "MacNeils Farewell to Barra."[83] The keeper of Kisimul took the family out to the castle in the bay for a private tour and offered them a bottle of Scotch from the shipwreck made famous by the movie *Whiskey Galore*.

Never much of a drinker, Stirling declined with thanks.

83   "MacNeil's Farewell to Barra" can be listened to at: https://www.youtube.com/watch?v=7GpsHW4xwqo

CAM AND HIS father bonded on a canoe trip when Campbell was a teenager.

In 1957, Dad, Randy Sterser and I embarked on a trip to deliver a freighter canoe from Peace River to Fort Vermillion, a distance of about 200 miles north. The first night we camped out was by a 'blow out,' natural gas burning from a pipe at what had been an oil well from the '20s. We had a campfire and could see the fire reflected in the yellow eyes of wolves that had come near us. Randy had a rifle and wanted to shoot the wolves but Dad said, 'They don't bother us so we won't bother them.'

Cam saw a very different side of his dad on that trip, the northern man. The next day they came to an Indigenous village where they met northern Cree who could not speak English. McNeil began to speak to them in Cree, a language he had not spoken since his days in the North 20 years before. When his dad started to speak in Cree, the children who had gathered rolled around on the ground, laughing. They thought it was the funniest thing. It was a real northern adventure and one of the great times Cam had with his dad.

IN THE SUMMER of 1971, 30 years after her father had left the North, Cam's sister Barbara was able to visit some of the places he had been posted. "It was a riverboat trip. We went from Fort Nelson to Fort Liard, Fort Simpson and to Fort Providence, all Dad's old stomping grounds." They even shot rapids on the Liard River.

I was introduced around the North as Big Mac's daughter and everybody would say 'Big Mac!' and they would start in on how they remembered him and what a good guy he was.

In Fort Providence she went in to buy some moccasins for her newborn nephew Stirling. The staff went and got a "little nun" who had been up there forever. "She came out and patted my hand and said she was so glad to see me. She said, 'Oh, I remember your father. He was a very brotherly man, a brotherly man.'" At Kraus Hot Springs, Barbara met Mary and Gus Kraus, the only known permanent residents of Nahanni National Park.[84] Mary gave her a painting to bring back for her dad.

He was thrilled.

CAMPBELL MCNEIL JOINED the RCMP as a Special Constable Seaman in 1959, just before he was 18. There were two ways you could join before the age of 18—one was to be a trumpeter, the other was to be in the "Marine" Division. Since he did not play trumpet, "Marine" Division it was. Cam found the RCMP exam harder than the Air Force exam to be an officer. He enjoyed the "Marine" Division because he was doing something useful—saving people's lives, pretty heady stuff for a kid of 17. An added bonus was that no one knew who Stirling McNeil was, and Cam could be gauged on his own merits.

It was when his father was transferred to Prince Edward Island that Cam went to Dalhousie University in Halifax, where

84 "Nahanni National Park Reserve of Canada," *Parks Canada*, http://www.pc.gc.ca/eng/pn-np/nt/nahanni/natcul/natcul2.aspx. Accessed March 21, 2016.

his university career included a stint with the Royal Canadian Air Force. At his graduation parade in St. Jean, PQ, Cam was surprised to see a familiar RCMP officer in blue on the reviewing stand. The Air Officer Commanding Training Command was a war-time friend of Stirling's and had sent a DC-3 to P.E.I. so he could attend his son's graduation.

As a Flight Cadet, Cam was posted to RCAF Station Parent, on the Pinetree Radar Line north of Québec City.

I was told to get my ass into my best uniform and report to the Chief Operations Officer on the Hill, which I did, and marched in, saluted and said, 'Flight Cadet McNeil reporting, sir.'

The Chief Operations Officer then told young Cam that McNeil had saved his life:

I was his pilot and he was in the back of the airplane. He saw me turn. We were in the mountains in the area of Castlegar, B.C. When I made the turn, your dad looked out the window and immediately yelled to get right over and turn around right now because it was a box canyon.

McNeil had recognized it while the pilot did not. It was a very foggy, rainy day with poor visibility, and they would have been killed had they continued. The Air Force Officer went on:

I am going to be very hard on you because I admired your dad. If you want to be my assistant, I'll work the ass off you but it will

be a really good summer for you because you'll be doing stuff that
most flying officers would never get involved in.

One of these jobs was Classified Books Officer, which required a "top secret" RCMP security clearance. A high priority wire was sent to "L" Division in P.E.I., his home province, and, of course, then under the command of none other than Supt. Stirling McNeil. Young Cam was told later by the Sergeant Major who had brought the file into Supt. McNeil's office in the midst of other files that he had said, "Sir, we need these right away, if you wouldn't mind." A number of people in the office knew what was happening and they thought they were going to pull a fast one on the boss. They were watching through the doors when he went through the files, signing them. "Then the Sergeant Major pulled out my file and asked if everything was all right." But McNeil didn't even crack a smile. "What are you people doing here? Get back to work," he told them. Well, perhaps he did so with just a hint of a grin.

Campbell McNeil was chosen for air crew in the Air Force and told he was one in fifty (son Stirling was one in five hundred when hired by the Ottawa Fire Department), but Cam was not allowed to be a pilot. He passed every exam but was too tall for the T33 trainer jets. Any attempt to eject from the front seat of the T33 would have taken his kneecaps off. It was devastating not to be an Air Force pilot like his dad. He was offered positions as a Navigator or Radio Officer, but declined and went back to his ground job as temporary Adjutant at Holberg. He later flew with 436 Squadron as an unofficial Navigator and in the T33.

CAM DECIDED TO get his pilot's license on his own, just as his dad had done back in the early 1930s. He bought his first airplane, a Piper Tripacer, the day before he graduated. His father was very pleased. George Dewar flew the plane north to Seven Islands and McNeil flew with Cam in that airplane "down North" via Edmonton and the Beaufort Sea to Victoria. By that time, his dad was retired and living at Brentwood Bay near Victoria, B.C. They flew down the Mackenzie River over McNeil's old territory, where he had been the engineer or mechanic on the Mounted Police boat down the Mackenzie, on patrol with dog teams, and travelled in both canoe and aircraft. McNeil had flown with pilot "Wop" May and "Punch" Dickens in G-CASK, one of the old Fokkers. He also flew with Russ Baker, the founder of Pacific Western Airlines. Although he did not fly with Max Ward, McNeil met him when he was a Sergeant Major in Edmonton.[85]

Mounted Police officers keep their rank after retirement. As Superintendent, McNeil was the senior officer in the Northwest Territories. As a result, whenever they landed along the Mackenzie, McNeil and Cam got VIP treatment, including being met by RCMP escorts from Hay River to Fort Simpson, each detachment radioing ahead.

In Hay River, people remembered McNeil, known for wearing a black sweatband and for having shot all the loose dogs in the town because a child had been killed by wild dogs. Before doing so,

---

85 "Maxwell William Ward ... joined the RCAF in 1940 and served as a flight instructor during WWII. Max Ward worked as a bush pilot after the war and made an out-standing contribution to the service of the northern frontier by air." Max Ward was the founder of Wardair. "Maxwell William Ward," Historica Canada, http://www.thecanadianencyclopedia.ca/en/article/maxwell-william-ward/. Accessed May 4, 2016.

McNeil had first gone around and told everybody to lock up their dogs. People in the North understood. Dogs are not pets. If they were not working, they were marauding. Other than target shooting, this was the only time in his career that he fired his revolver.[86] He only drew his weapon two other times, both in the '30s, once to break up a gang of toughs threatening to beat him up when he was alone on patrol, and once when he was escorting a mental patient who went wild and almost overpowered him.

Cam and his father had a wonderful time on that trip and McNeil's recollections were spot on.

We'd go along the river and he would say, 'See that snye there?[87] *We had a fuel cache in there and we'd land the Norseman right there.'*

When they got to Inuvik, Cam and McNeil went to the RCMP detachment to say hello, something they did in every community. McNeil started to ask about Special Constables, the Indigenous people who always helped the Force. Someone told him there was an ex-member dying in hospital. McNeil went to the hospital to visit the dying man, whose wife was at his bedside. He told her, "Your husband was one of the best trackers and dogsled people on the whole river." She was pleased that the Superintendent remembered her husband. McNeil then asked how the RCMP had been treating them. She replied, "Oh, we haven't heard from the RCMP."

McNeil seldom got angry but when he did, he was formidable.

---

86   McNeil was a good shot, earning the crossed revolvers and crossed rifles worn on his uniform sleeve.

87   A backwater.

McNeil left the hospital at a fast clip, headed for the detachment. He went right through to the Sub-Division Commander. He didn't slam the door, but Cam knew the CO had been given a piece of his father's mind. McNeil came out, took a deep breath and they carried on, leaving Inuvik that day. The former Special Constable died a couple of days later, and the Mounted Police had a full contingent at the funeral in red serge.

McNeil valued his relationship with Indigenous people; the Mounted Police could not have done their jobs without them. And McNeil himself would probably have perished had it not been for the Special Constables who knew the country and knew how to survive. On one occasion, McNeil cut his leg badly when the axe he was wielding bounced off a frozen tree, but the Special Constable stopped the bleeding and got him to Fort Providence. The Mounted Police didn't give their men enough supplies to last through the winter. They had to hunt—and particularly to fish, especially for the dogs—for enough to last the year. And who better than Indigenous people knew how to hunt and fish in the barrens and the North? McNeil did so much fishing for the dogs that it was ever after a pastime he did not enjoy. Everyone in the small communities of the North knew to behave or they would be sentenced to the RCMP fish camp to do hard work.

The side trip from Fort Simpson to Fort Nelson via the Nahanni was one of the best, and scariest, flights of Cam McNeil's life. It began badly when large, clever ravens stole breakfast from the sleeping tent under the wing of the Tripacer. "The scenery was magnificent, but we almost had a collision with another aircraft over Virginia Falls.[88] The low level flight down the Nahanni in the canyons was very memorable."

Another flight that brought back memories was the one from Ottawa to Toronto Cam shared with his father in the Mooney in instrument conditions. They were in the clouds for the whole trip. Stirling was an excellent visual flyer but had never learned to fly on instruments, and kept asking if Cam knew where he was. Cam did. The Toronto International Runway 24R lights appeared right where and when they should have, and Stirling was relieved.

THE McNEILS' FOUR grandchildren also had great love and admiration for their grandparents. McNeil took great pride in both Barbara's sons, Liard (Lee) and Jonathan, and was very pleased to pin Air Cadet's wings on Lee, who received a Glider Wing at the age of 16 and the Fixed Wing at age 18.

Lee said it was a proud day for both he and his grandfather when he received his pilot's wings. Lee had learned to fly in a Cessna 172, having received a scholarship from the Air Cadets, where he rose to the rank of Flight Sergeant. He and his friends would sometimes fly into the mountains behind Chilliwack and Abbotsford, B.C. where they would practice dogfights and aerobatics. No doubt his grandfather didn't know about that.

Lee loved to take his grandfather for rides and took him to events like Remembrance Day ceremonies. On one occasion he took him to see the famed *St. Roch*, now part of the Maritime Museum in Vancouver. He knew that his grandfather had been

---

88   Virginia Falls is twice as high as Niagara Falls.

acquainted with *St. Roch*'s skipper, Supt. Henry Larsen, and thought how strange it must be for his grandfather to see the famous RCMP vessel in a museum.

McNeil always called Lee by his proper name, Liard, with emphasis on the last syllable. His uncle, Campbell Stirling Liard McNeil, also carried the name that came from Stirling McNeil's love of the North and Fort Liard on the Liard River, his first command.

"I was very proud to be his grandson," Lee said.

There is no doubt McNeil was proud of all his grandchildren: Lee and Jonathan, as well as Stirling and Melissa, Cam's children.

Jon recalled his grandfather having many stories and loving to talk to people. When McNeil moved to Langley, he would walk up and down the road with his cane and wave at every car that went by. All kinds of people knew him just from his walks up and down the road. "When he died," Barbara said, "we put the flag on the flagpole at half-mast, and many people felt bereft. They realized the lowered flag was for him."

And McNeil was obsessed with the mail, which Barbara believed stemmed from his many years in the North where the mail only arrived once every two or three months. She said, "I'm sure his staff wondered why the first thing he had to do wherever he was posted was to go down to the post office and get the mail." As recalled by many others, when Supt. McNeil was the Officer Commanding Prince Edward Island, he would drive to downtown Charlottetown from RCMP headquarters to get the mail, parking downtown and then going up and down the street, chatting with those he met on his way.

There is great pride in the McNeil legacy. Grandson Stirling and his wife Nicole have three children: Garrett Stirling (named for his father, grandfather and great-grandfather)[89]; Paige; and Chloe.

"When I was playing baseball," grandson Stirling said, "[my grandfather] would be right behind the backstop, cheering." His grandparents once looked after him for a week while his parents were away. There was some question of grandfather's ability to drive because of his age. Had he not been able to, young Stirling would have missed his ball game. Grandfather said "nuts to that" and took him to the game, transmission grinding all the way.

Four generations of Stirling McNeils: Campbell Stirling Liard, Alexander Stirling, Stirling Asaph, and Garret Stirling.

Stirling last saw his grandfather a few months before he died.

He had just lost his second leg and it was tough on him since he was a proud man. Grandmother had died. But he still had his sense of humour. I remember a couple of veterans—who had been rookies when he was the CO in Charlottetown—visiting him. He joked 'It's lucky I got into the RCMP when I did because they wouldn't take me now. I wouldn't make the height requirement'!

---

89 Garrett Stirling received an A for his school report "A Giant Among Men—The Storied Life of My Great-Grandfather."

Melissa felt her grandparents were a huge influence on her life:

Grandma was the loveliest, most considerate, most gracious woman you could ever meet, but if you ever criticized her husband or her family, she turned into 'lady tiger.' Granddad was such a gentleman, so funny, so much fun to all his grandkids. He would make funny faces at lunch, wink at us while pretending to listen to my father.

Melissa's oldest daughter is named Carolyn, after her grandmother; her son is Alexander Stirling, after her grandfather; and her youngest daughter is Catharine Uldine.

CAM HAD THESE final thoughts about his father:

The mark of the man was not how he handled his many successes, but how he faced—head on—life's reverses. He didn't dwell on the past. He looked for the best in people and situations and usually found it. He went from the rank of RCAF Wing Commander to RCMP Corporal with dignity, equanimity and enthusiasm for the new challenge. At the end of his life, he handled considerable pain and anguish without complaint.

…my father and his peers…believed that you gave to, not got out of, the Force—and, indeed, life. By giving selflessly, with no thought of reward, they received a very rich and fulfilling life. This, in a nutshell, is his lesson and his legacy.

EPILOGUE 2: THE LEGACY

The McNeil Shield and Sports Day

FOUR YEARS AFTER his death, the RCMP announced creation of the "McNeil Shield for Excellence Program" and the Stirling McNeil Sports Day at "Depot" Division.

The McNeil Shield and Sports Day honour the memory of Supt. McNeil, who served from 1931 until his retirement in 1966. They encourage academic excellence, teamwork, leadership and *esprit de corps* among cadet troops in training at "Depot" Division in Regina. Much of the spadework in creating the McNeil Shield was done by McNeil's son, Cam, and Supt. Greg Peters, Director of the RCMP Strategic Partnership and Heritage Branch.[90]

The Shield is championed by serving members and veterans of the RCMP, as well as fellow public historians. The Sports Day is an initiative of "Depot" Staff.

Cadets are encouraged to participate as teams in various organized sporting events. Cadets and troops are evaluated on academic excellence, teamwork, leadership, *esprit de corps* and in maintaining

---

90   Supt. Peters, MVO is now Usher of the Black Rod, the senior parliamentary protocol officer. He was awarded Member of the Royal Victorian Order by Her Majesty in a private investiture—just the Queen and his family. The Queen calls him "Greg."

Supt. Alexander Stirling McNeil KSt.J MiD

Stirling McNeil believed in doing his duty for God, the Queen, Canada, the Force and his family. He believed in a healthy mind in a healthy body. He was a man's man – while in Depot he played for the 1931 Regina Roughriders and again in 1937 after four years of hard northern service. He was a boxing champion. He kept fit into his nineties.

He served his country in peace and war – he joined the reserve army at 17, then the force for 35 years. When war was declared, he was flying the first RCMP aircraft in the north. He transferred to the Royal Canadian Air Force. At the end of the war he was a Wing Commander, decorated with Mentioned in Dispatches, Director of Security and Intelligence for Western Air Command and a star of the RCAF rugby team.

He was a policeman's policeman. From the Air Force he returned as a Corporal to a one-man detachment in Young, Sask. He rose by hard work and caring about and for the people he dealt with to be S/M in "K", then Adgt. and Training Officer at Depot, O/C 1952 Musical Ride, Canadian Representative to the U.S. Navy DEW Line Task Force, on standby to head RCMP peacekeepers for Cyprus which were never sent, O/C Peace River Subdivision and, finally, C/O "L" Division. When he retired, he was asked to be Lt.Gov. of PEI, but could not afford the entertaining on his pension.

In his retirement, he headed every major veteran's organization in Victoria and many others. He was knighted when he was 80.

The McNeil Shield, with description. *Photograph courtesy of RCMP Academy "Depot" Division.*

the core values of the RCMP: honesty, integrity, professionalism, compassion, accountability and respect.

The McNeil Shield winners receive a silver medallion with the likeness of Supt. McNeil on one side and the Force crest on the other. It simply states, "McNeil Shield for Excellence."

ACKNOWLEDGMENTS

THE AUTHOR WISHES to thank a number of people for their invaluable assistance. My sincere gratitude goes to Al Nicholson and the RCMP Heritage Centre for their kind assistance in ensuring the publication of this book, and to Henry Purdy, the visual artist whose portrait of Stirling McNeil appears on the front cover.

Stirling McNeil's son, Cam McNeil, was instrumental in helping with family history, as was his sister, Barbara Price. Cam offered useful suggestions, insights and corrections. Editor Heather Nickel was tenacious in her quest for accuracy and verification of sources.

Supt. Ernie MacAulay (Rtd.) acted as technical advisor and editor. The author is also indebted to former Supt. Greg Peters (Rtd.), RCMP Heritage Branch, and his staff for their interest in and support of this project. A/Comm. Fraser MacRae (Rtd.), OIC Surrey Detachment, was helpful in gaining assistance from *The Quarterly*, from retired A/Commr. Allen Burchill's e-mail newsletter, and from his father, Supt. Bill MacRae (Rtd.).

Scarlet & Gold, published by the RCMP Veteran's Association, was also very helpful. In fact, the suggestion for writing this book was made by Sgt. Ron Budd (Rtd.), who had read an account of the McNeil Shield in *Scarlet & Gold*. S/Sgt. Bob McKee (Rtd.), then-president, Vancouver Branch, RCMP Veterans Association, secured the loan of eight boxes of material, including copies of *The Quarterly* and *Scarlet & Gold* going back several years, along with other memorabilia, including letters written by Stirling McNeil.

The author conducted a series of interviews by phone and in person, and corresponded by e-mail with many retired members of the Force. Thanks to: Howard "Hap" Armstrong, Bob Brownlee, Gus Buziak, Vince Cain, Ralph Cave, Gar Clark, Colin Craig, Robert Dempster, George Dewar, Don Duke, John Entwistle, Jim Forsyth, Garth Hampson, Dave Holmes, Dan Lemieux, Ernie MacAulay, Cliff MacDonald, Cort MacDonell, Carl MacLeod, Marshall MacKinnon, Dick McLaren, Joe Naaykens, Harry Nixon, Fred Rhodes, Murray Ross, Randy Schramm, Bill Schindeler, Bill Stephens, Jack Thornton and Don Wilson.

Others interviewed were: Stephen Price, Stirling McNeil's son-in-law who is also a retired member; Rev. Pam Worthington; Army Lt.-Col. Cecil Berezowski (Rtd.); Navy Lt.-Comm. Stirling Ross (Rtd.); two civilian employees of the RCMP, Bonnie Schneider and Lainie Goddard; and long-time family friend, Esther Farr, widow of A/Comm. Terry Farr. The author also spoke to all four McNeil grandchildren: Stirling McNeil and Melissa Kane, both of Ottawa; and Lee and Jonathan Price.

The author is indebted to Anne Schroeder, who provided personal care to both Supt. and Mrs. McNeil in their latter years.

SOURCES

"Adventures of McNeil of the Mounties,"
David Guy (*Ottawa Citizen*, July 21, 2001).

The Death of Albert Johnson: Mad Trapper of Rat River
Frank W. Anderson (Victoria, B.C.: Heritage House, 2011).

Keepers of the Law
Regina and District Old Timers' Association,
(Regina and District Old Timers' Association, 2005).

The Mad Trapper: The Incredible Tale of a Famous Canadian Manhunt
Helena Katz (Canmore, AB: Altitude Publishing, 2004).

One Canada: Memoirs of the Right Honourable John G. Diefenbaker
John Diefenbaker (Macmillan, 1975).

The Red Wall: A Woman in the RCMP
Jane Hall, (General Store Publishing House, 2007).

The Way It Was: 50 Years of RCMP Memories
Don Saul, ed. (Victoria Division RCMP Veterans Association, 1990).

Wings of a Hero: Canadian Pioneer Flying Ace Wilfrid Wop May
Sheila Reid (St. Catherines, ON: Vanwell Publishing, 1998).

Scarlet & Gold
The Canadian Press
The National Post
The Quarterly

Photo credit: Lianne Watt

ABOUT THE AUTHOR

GEORGE GARRETT IS a veteran of nearly 50 years in broadcast journalism. Throughout his career he worked closely with many police officers and gained their trust by endeavouring to deal with them fairly, without prejudicing an investigation, while keeping the public informed at the same time. Garrett has won a number of awards, including lifetime achievement awards from the Radio & TV News Directors of Canada and from the Jack Webster Foundation in Vancouver. He was twice named Broadcast Performer of the Year by the B.C. Association of Broadcasters.

George Garrett is the most credible and trustworthy journalist I have ever met. He has had an exceptional relationship with the Force during his journalistic career.

—Supt. Ernie MacAulay (Rtd.)

Garrett was named an Honorary Member of the RCMP Veteran's Association, Vancouver Branch in 1993, and made a Life Member in 2013.